Python Data Wrangling for Business Analytics

Python for Business Analytics Series

George Snypes

Published by Northwood Lore Books, 2024.

PYTHON DATA WRANGLING FOR BUSINESS ANALYTICS

First edition. November 18, 2024.

ISBN: 979-8230433927

Written by George Snypes.

Table of Contents

1. Introduction to Data Wrangling in Business Context 1
2. Setting Up Your Python Environment for Data Analysis 5
3. Understanding Business Data: Types and Structures 9
4. Pandas Fundamentals for Business Analytics 13
5. NumPy Essentials for Data Processing 17
6. Reading and Writing Data: Multiple File Formats 21
7. Basic Data Cleaning Operations 25
8. Handling Missing Data in Business Datasets 29
9. Data Validation Fundamentals 33
10. Building Data Quality Frameworks 37
11. String Operations and Text Cleaning 41
12. Date and Time Data Processing 45
13. Numerical Data Preprocessing 49
14. Categorical Data Handling 53
15. Advanced Data Transformation Techniques 57
16. Reshaping and Pivoting Data 61
17. Aggregation Methods for Business Metrics 64
18. Merging and Joining Datasets 68
19. Complex Dataset Integration 72
20. Time Series Data Fundamentals 76
21. Time Series Analysis for Business 80
22. Seasonal Decomposition and Trending 84
23. Customer Data Processing 88
24. Customer Segmentation Techniques 92
25. Sales Data Transformation 96
26. Sales Performance Analytics 100
27. Financial Data Cleaning 104
28. Financial Reporting Automation 108
29. Marketing Campaign Data Processing 112
30. Marketing Analytics Workflows 116
31. Supply Chain Data Integration 120

32. Operations Data Management 124
33. API Data Collection and Processing 128
34. Working with Database Connections 132
35. Cloud Data Sources Integration 136
36. Excel to Python Migration Strategies 140
37. Automated Data Validation Systems 144
38. Building ETL Pipelines 148
39. Data Pipeline Optimization 152
40. Performance Tuning for Large Datasets 156
41. Memory Optimization Techniques 160
42. Parallel Processing in Python 164
43. Error Handling and Debugging 168
44. Code Documentation Best Practices 172
45. Testing Data Wrangling Code 176
46. Version Control for Data Projects 180
47. Reproducible Analysis Workflows 184
48. Automated Reporting Systems 188
49. Data Visualization Preparation 192
50. Dashboard Data Processing 196
51. Real-time Data Processing 200
52. Data Privacy and Security 204
53. Best Practices in Production 208
54. Case Studies and Real-world Applications 212

1. Introduction to Data Wrangling in Business Context

Data wrangling has become an indispensable skill in today's business landscape, where organizations are inundated with vast amounts of raw data that need to be transformed into actionable insights. As businesses increasingly rely on data-driven decision making, the ability to efficiently clean, process, and prepare data for analysis has become a crucial competency for analysts, data scientists, and business professionals alike. This chapter sets the foundation for understanding data wrangling in a business context and explores why Python has emerged as the tool of choice for modern data processing workflows.

In the contemporary business environment, data comes from numerous sources and in various formats. Customer relationship management systems generate detailed interaction logs, point-of-sale systems record transaction data, web analytics tools track user behavior, and IoT devices stream continuous operational metrics. This diversity of data sources presents both opportunities and challenges. While the potential for extracting valuable business insights is immense, the raw data often requires significant preprocessing before it can be meaningfully analyzed. This is where data wrangling becomes essential.

Data wrangling, also known as data preprocessing or data preparation, encompasses all the activities involved in transforming raw data into a format suitable for analysis. These activities include cleaning inconsistent or incorrect data, handling missing values, standardizing formats, combining data from multiple sources, and creating derived variables that better represent the underlying business concepts. In a business context, effective data wrangling can mean the difference between making informed decisions based on reliable analysis and drawing incorrect conclusions from flawed data.

Python has established itself as the premier language for data wrangling tasks, offering several advantages that make it particularly well-suited for business analytics. First, Python's extensive ecosystem of data processing libraries, particularly pandas and NumPy, provides powerful tools for handling structured data. These libraries offer intuitive interfaces for common data manipulation tasks while maintaining the performance necessary for processing large datasets. Second, Python's readable syntax and extensive documentation make it accessible to professionals transitioning from other tools like Excel or SQL. Third, Python's versatility allows it to integrate seamlessly with various data sources and analytical tools, making it an ideal choice for end-to-end data processing pipelines.

The business impact of effective data wrangling cannot be overstated. Consider a retail company analyzing customer purchasing patterns to optimize inventory management. The raw data might include transaction records from multiple store locations, each using slightly different formats for product codes and customer IDs. Some transactions might have missing timestamps, while others contain obvious errors like negative quantities. Before any meaningful analysis can begin, this data must be cleaned and standardized. A well-designed data wrangling process can automate these cleanup tasks, ensuring consistency across analyses and freeing analysts to focus on extracting insights rather than managing data quality issues.

Financial services provide another compelling example of the importance of data wrangling. Banks and investment firms deal with massive volumes of transaction data, market feeds, and customer information. These datasets often contain sensitive information that must be handled securely while being transformed into formats suitable for risk analysis, fraud detection, or regulatory reporting. Python's data wrangling capabilities allow financial analysts to create reproducible workflows that maintain data integrity while automating routine preprocessing tasks.

Marketing departments increasingly rely on data wrangling to integrate customer data from multiple touchpoints. Social media interactions, email campaign responses, website behavior, and offline purchase history must be combined to create a comprehensive view of customer behavior. This integration requires careful handling of different data formats, resolution of conflicting information, and creation of consistent customer identifiers across platforms. Python's data wrangling tools excel at these tasks, enabling marketers to build accurate customer profiles and measure campaign effectiveness across channels.

The importance of data quality cannot be overemphasized in business analytics. Poor data quality can lead to incorrect conclusions and misguided business decisions. Data wrangling plays a crucial role in implementing data quality controls and validation procedures. Through automated checks and cleaning procedures, organizations can ensure their analyses are based on reliable, consistent data. This is particularly important in regulated industries where data accuracy has legal implications, such as healthcare or financial services.

As organizations move toward automated decision-making systems and machine learning applications, the role of data wrangling becomes even more critical. Machine learning models are only as good as the data they're trained on, making proper data preparation essential for successful AI initiatives. Python's data wrangling capabilities integrate seamlessly with popular machine learning libraries, allowing organizations to build end-to-end analytical pipelines that maintain data quality throughout the modeling process.

Efficiency and scalability are key considerations in business data wrangling. As dataset sizes grow and analysis requirements become more complex, organizations need tools that can handle increased processing demands while maintaining performance. Python's data wrangling libraries are designed to handle large datasets efficiently, with options for parallel processing and memory optimization when needed. This scalability ensures that data processing workflows can grow with an organization's needs.

The future of business data wrangling is evolving with the emergence of new data sources and analytical requirements. Real-time data processing, integration with cloud services, and automated pipeline management are becoming increasingly important. Python's active development community and extensive ecosystem ensure that new tools and capabilities are continuously being developed to meet these emerging needs.

Throughout this book, we will explore these aspects of data wrangling in detail, providing practical examples and techniques that you can apply in your own business analytics work. We'll begin with fundamental data cleaning and transformation techniques, progress through advanced data integration and pipeline development, and conclude with best practices for maintaining and scaling data processing workflows. Whether you're analyzing customer behavior, optimizing operations, or automating financial reporting, the skills you'll learn will enable you to handle real-world data challenges effectively and efficiently.

The journey through data wrangling is both technical and strategic. While mastering the technical tools is important, understanding how to apply them in a business context is equally crucial. We'll emphasize not just the "how" of data wrangling, but also the "why," ensuring you can make informed decisions about data preprocessing strategies that align with your organization's goals and requirements.

2. Setting Up Your Python Environment for Data Analysis

Setting up a proper Python environment is the crucial first step in your data wrangling journey. This chapter will guide you through establishing a robust, professional-grade development environment that will serve as the foundation for your business analytics work.

The Python ecosystem offers numerous options for setting up your development environment, and choosing the right combination of tools is essential for productive data analysis. We'll focus on creating a setup that balances ease of use with professional capabilities, ensuring you can handle everything from quick exploratory analysis to production-grade data processing.

Anaconda has emerged as the de facto standard distribution for data analytics work in Python. This comprehensive platform includes not only Python itself but also hundreds of pre-installed packages commonly used in data science and business analytics. Installing Anaconda provides you with a complete environment including essential libraries like pandas, NumPy, matplotlib, and scikit-learn, along with the powerful Jupyter notebook interface for interactive analysis.

While Anaconda provides an excellent starting point, understanding virtual environments is crucial for maintaining clean, reproducible analysis workflows. Virtual environments allow you to create isolated Python installations for different projects, each with its own set of dependencies. This isolation prevents conflicts between package versions and makes it easier to share your analysis with colleagues. The conda environment manager, included with Anaconda, provides robust tools for creating and managing these environments.

Creating your first virtual environment is straightforward with conda. Open your terminal or command prompt and enter: conda create -n business_analytics python=3.9. This command creates a new environment named "business_analytics" using Python 3.9. After activation with conda activate business_analytics, you can install additional packages specific to your project without affecting other Python installations on your system.

For business analytics work, several key packages should be installed in your environment. Beyond the core data processing libraries (pandas and NumPy), consider installing packages for data visualization (matplotlib, seaborn), statistical analysis (scipy, statsmodels), and database connectivity (sqlalchemy, psycopg2). The command conda install pandas numpy matplotlib seaborn scipy statsmodels sqlalchemy will set up most of these essential tools.

Integrated Development Environments (IDEs) play a crucial role in productive Python development. While Jupyter notebooks are excellent for exploratory analysis and documentation, a full-featured IDE provides additional tools for code development and debugging. VS Code has become increasingly popular among data professionals, offering excellent Python support through its extensions. PyCharm, particularly its Professional edition, provides specialized features for data science work, including advanced database tools and scientific mode for working with notebooks.

Setting up VS Code for Python development involves installing several extensions. The Python extension provides basic language support, while the Jupyter extension enables notebook functionality within the editor. The Python Interactive window feature combines the immediacy of notebooks with the power of a full IDE. Additional extensions like Python Test Explorer and Python Docstring Generator help maintain code quality and documentation.

Git version control is essential for managing your analysis code professionally. While GUI tools are available, learning basic git commands helps you understand the version control process better. Configure git with your credentials using git config—global user.name

"Your Name" and git config—global user.email "your.email@example.com". Create a .gitignore file in your project directory to exclude large data files, sensitive information, and environment-specific files from version control.

Organizing your project structure consistently helps maintain clean, maintainable code. A typical data analysis project might include directories for raw data, processed data, notebooks for exploration, source code for reusable functions, and documentation. Consider using a project template to ensure consistency across different analyses. The cookiecutter data science project template provides a well-thought-out structure that many organizations adopt as their standard.

For handling sensitive business data, proper security configurations are essential. Ensure your Python environment variables are set up to handle credentials securely. The python-dotenv package allows you to store sensitive information like database passwords in a .env file that isn't committed to version control. Install it with pip install python-dotenv and create a .env file to store your configuration variables.

Performance considerations should influence your environment setup, particularly when working with large datasets. Configure your pandas options for optimal memory usage: pd.set_option('mode.chained_assignment', None) reduces unnecessary warnings, while pd.set_option('display.max_columns', None) helps during exploratory analysis. For very large datasets, consider installing packages like dask or vaex that provide out-of-memory computation capabilities.

Code formatting and style consistency contribute to maintainable analysis code. Install the black code formatter (pip install black) and configure your IDE to apply it automatically. The flake8 linter helps catch potential errors and style violations before they cause problems. Consider adding a pre-commit hook to automatically check code formatting before commits.

Jupyter notebook extensions can significantly enhance your analytical workflow. The jupyter_contrib_nbextensions package provides useful features like table of contents generation, code folding, and execution timing. Install it with pip install jupyter_contrib_nbextensions and jupyter contrib nbextension install—user to enable these capabilities.

Documentation tools help maintain clear records of your analysis process. Install Sphinx (pip install sphinx) for generating professional documentation from your code comments. The nbconvert tool, included with Jupyter, allows you to convert notebooks to various formats for sharing results with stakeholders.

Regular environment maintenance ensures stable, reproducible analysis. Periodically update your packages with conda update—all, but do so in a controlled manner to avoid breaking changes. Keep a requirements.txt or environment.yml file updated to record your environment's exact package versions.

The environment you create today will support your data wrangling work throughout this book and beyond. Take time to set it up thoughtfully, documenting your choices and configurations. A well-configured Python environment makes the difference between struggling with technical issues and focusing on meaningful data analysis that drives business value.

3. Understanding Business Data: Types and Structures

Understanding business data types and structures forms the foundation of effective data wrangling in Python. Before diving into complex transformations and analysis, analysts must develop a clear understanding of how business data is organized, stored, and represented in various formats.

Business data comes in many shapes and sizes, each with its own characteristics and challenges. At the most fundamental level, we encounter scalar data types that represent single values. These include numeric data like sales figures, prices, and inventory counts, which can be integers or floating-point numbers depending on the need for decimal precision. Text data, represented as strings, captures everything from product descriptions and customer names to transaction IDs and status codes. Boolean values track binary states like order fulfillment status or customer activity flags. Dates and timestamps record crucial temporal information about business events, from transaction times to delivery schedules.

Moving beyond individual values, business data is typically organized into structured formats that capture relationships and hierarchies. Tables, the most common structure in business analytics, organize data into rows and columns. Each row represents an observation or record, while columns contain attributes or features of those records. For example, a sales table might have rows for individual transactions and columns for date, product ID, quantity, price, and customer information.

Hierarchical data structures appear frequently in business contexts. Organization charts, product categories, and geographic groupings often follow tree-like structures where items have parent-child relationships. This hierarchical nature can be represented in various ways, from nested dictionaries in Python to specialized formats like JSON or XML. Understanding these relationships is crucial for tasks like rolling up sales figures by region or analyzing performance across different organizational levels.

Time series data structures deserve special attention in business analytics. Many business metrics, from daily sales figures to stock prices, follow temporal patterns. Time series data typically combines timestamps with one or more measured values, often including additional dimensions like product categories or regional breakdowns. This data structure requires specific handling techniques to account for time-based relationships, seasonality, and trends.

Categorical data appears throughout business datasets, representing discrete groups or classifications. This might include customer segments, product categories, or status codes. Categories can be nominal (without inherent order, like product types) or ordinal (with meaningful order, like customer satisfaction ratings). Understanding the nature of categorical data is essential for choosing appropriate analysis methods and ensuring meaningful aggregations.

Sparse data structures often emerge in business contexts, particularly in areas like customer behavior analysis or product recommendations. These structures efficiently represent datasets where most possible combinations have no value, such as customer purchase histories across thousands of possible products. Understanding how to work with sparse representations can significantly impact the efficiency of your analysis.

Network data structures capture relationships between entities in your business data. Customer referral networks, supply chain relationships, and social media interactions all follow network patterns. These structures typically represent connections as edges between nodes, requiring specialized handling techniques for analysis and visualization.

Modern business data often includes unstructured or semi-structured elements. Text fields in customer feedback, email communications, or social media posts require natural language processing techniques. Image data from product photos or security cameras needs specialized handling. Understanding how to integrate these unstructured elements with traditional structured data is increasingly important.

Data quality characteristics are integral to understanding business data structures. Missing values, a common challenge in business datasets, can take various forms: truly missing information, intentionally blank fields, or invalid entries. Understanding the patterns and reasons for missing data helps inform appropriate handling strategies.

Business data often includes derived or calculated fields that depend on other values. Understanding these dependencies is crucial for maintaining data integrity and ensuring accurate analysis. For example, total order value might be calculated from quantity and unit price, while customer lifetime value combines multiple transaction records.

Data granularity varies across business contexts and needs careful consideration. Transaction-level data provides the most detail but can be unwieldy for high-level analysis. Aggregated data reduces volume but loses detail. Understanding the appropriate level of granularity for different analyses helps balance accuracy with efficiency.

Security and privacy considerations influence how business data is structured and accessed. Personal identifying information might be encrypted or tokenized, requiring special handling in analysis. Understanding these security structures ensures compliance while maintaining analytical capabilities.

Business data often comes with implicit assumptions and business rules that affect its interpretation. Order dates might exclude weekends, prices might include or exclude tax depending on region, and customer categories might follow specific classification rules. Documenting and understanding these business rules is crucial for accurate analysis.

Data consistency and standardization pose ongoing challenges in business analytics. The same information might be represented differently across systems: dates in various formats, product codes with different conventions, or customer names with inconsistent capitalization. Understanding these variations is essential for data integration and cleaning.

Version control and historical tracking add another dimension to business data structures. Many systems maintain audit trails or historical records, tracking changes to important business data over time. Understanding how this historical information is structured enables accurate temporal analysis and compliance reporting.

The scale of business data influences structure choices. While small datasets might fit comfortably in memory as pandas DataFrames, larger datasets might require streaming processing or distributed storage. Understanding these scaling considerations helps in choosing appropriate tools and techniques.

Finally, business data rarely exists in isolation. External data sources, from market indicators to weather data, often need to be integrated with internal business data. Understanding how to align and combine data structures from different sources while maintaining consistency and meaning is a crucial skill in business analytics.

As we progress through this book, this foundational understanding of business data types and structures will inform our choices of tools and techniques for effective data wrangling. Each structure presents its own challenges and opportunities, requiring different approaches for cleaning, transformation, and analysis. Keep these fundamental concepts in mind as we explore more advanced data wrangling techniques in subsequent chapters.

4. Pandas Fundamentals for Business Analytics

Pandas represents one of the most powerful and essential tools in the Python ecosystem for business analytics. Its rich functionality and intuitive interface make it the go-to library for data manipulation and analysis in business contexts. Understanding Pandas fundamentals sets the foundation for effective data wrangling and analysis throughout your analytics journey.

At its core, Pandas provides two primary data structures: Series and DataFrame. A Series is a one-dimensional labeled array that can hold data of any type, similar to a single column in a spreadsheet. DataFrames extend this concept to two dimensions, providing a tabular structure with rows and columns that business analysts will find familiar from their experience with spreadsheets and databases.

Creating DataFrames forms the starting point of most business analysis tasks. You can construct DataFrames from various sources: dictionaries, lists, numpy arrays, or external files. For business applications, a common pattern involves creating DataFrames from structured data sources like CSV files, Excel spreadsheets, or database queries. The DataFrame structure naturally maps to business data, with each row typically representing a transaction, customer, or other business entity, and columns containing the attributes or metrics associated with these entities.

Indexing and selecting data in Pandas follows multiple paradigms that provide flexibility in accessing and manipulating your business data. The loc accessor allows label-based indexing, while iloc provides integer-based indexing. These tools become particularly valuable when filtering specific customer segments, analyzing date ranges, or focusing on particular product categories. Column selection can be performed using single labels, lists of labels, or boolean conditions, enabling complex data filtering operations common in business analysis.

Data exploration in Pandas starts with basic methods that provide insights into your dataset's structure and content. The head() and tail() methods show the first and last rows, while info() provides a summary of data types and missing values. These quick checks help identify potential data quality issues early in the analysis process. The describe() method generates statistical summaries of numerical columns, offering immediate insights into metrics like average sales, price ranges, or customer behavior patterns.

Boolean indexing represents a powerful feature for business analysis, allowing you to filter data based on complex conditions. For example, you might need to identify high-value customers, filter transactions within specific date ranges, or focus on particular product categories. Combining multiple conditions using logical operators enables sophisticated filtering that matches real business requirements.

Handling missing data becomes straightforward with Pandas' built-in methods. The isnull() and notnull() functions help identify missing values, while fillna() offers various strategies for handling them. Business data often contains missing values for valid reasons: customers who haven't made a purchase, products without ratings, or optional survey responses. Pandas provides flexible approaches to handle these situations, from simple value replacement to more sophisticated forward or backward filling methods.

Data transformation operations form a crucial part of business analytics workflows. Pandas offers numerous methods for modifying data types, creating calculated fields, and applying functions across datasets. The astype() method converts columns to appropriate data types, ensuring proper handling of numerical calculations or string operations. The apply() function enables custom transformations, while map() facilitates value mapping and categorization tasks common in business analysis.

Grouping and aggregation capabilities in Pandas support essential business analysis tasks like sales reporting, customer segmentation, and performance analysis. The groupby() operation, combined with aggregation functions, enables quick calculation of business metrics across various dimensions. For example, you can easily compute total sales by region, average order value by customer segment, or product performance metrics across time periods.

Time series functionality in Pandas deserves special attention for business applications. The library provides robust support for working with dates and times, including specialized indexing, resampling, and rolling calculations. These features prove invaluable when analyzing sales trends, customer behavior patterns, or seasonal variations in business metrics.

String operations in Pandas facilitate text data processing, a common requirement in business analytics. The str accessor provides methods for string manipulation, pattern matching, and extraction. These capabilities help standardize product descriptions, clean customer names, or extract information from unstructured text fields.

Categorical data handling in Pandas offers memory-efficient storage and specialized operations for dealing with categorical variables common in business data. Customer segments, product categories, or status codes can be efficiently represented as categorical data types, improving both performance and analytical capabilities.

Memory management becomes important when working with large business datasets. Pandas provides tools to optimize memory usage through appropriate data type selection and efficient data structures. Understanding these optimization techniques helps build scalable analysis solutions that can handle growing business datasets.

Method chaining in Pandas enables clean and readable code by combining multiple operations. This approach proves particularly valuable when building data transformation pipelines that need to be maintainable and understandable by other analysts or stakeholders.

Performance considerations play a crucial role in business analytics applications. Pandas offers vectorized operations that perform efficiently on large datasets. Understanding when to use vectorized operations versus explicit loops can significantly impact the performance of your analysis workflows.

Integration with other Python libraries extends Pandas' capabilities. Numpy provides the foundation for numerical operations, while visualization libraries like Matplotlib and Seaborn work seamlessly with Pandas structures to create business insights. This ecosystem approach enables comprehensive analysis solutions that meet diverse business requirements.

Error handling in Pandas requires attention to ensure robust business applications. Understanding common errors and their solutions helps build reliable analysis workflows. Proper error handling includes checking for data type mismatches, handling missing values appropriately, and validating calculations.

As we progress through more advanced topics in this book, these Pandas fundamentals will serve as building blocks for sophisticated data wrangling solutions. The library's combination of powerful functionality and intuitive interface makes it an indispensable tool for modern business analytics.

5. NumPy Essentials for Data Processing

NumPy stands as a cornerstone library in Python's scientific computing ecosystem, providing essential functionality for efficient data processing and numerical operations crucial to business analytics. Understanding NumPy's capabilities enables analysts to handle large datasets efficiently and perform complex calculations with remarkable speed.

At its foundation, NumPy introduces the ndarray (n-dimensional array) object, which offers significant advantages over traditional Python lists for numerical computations. These arrays provide a uniform data type structure that enables vectorized operations, eliminating the need for explicit loops and dramatically improving performance. In business analytics, this translates to faster processing of large financial datasets, customer behavior matrices, or sales performance arrays.

Array creation in NumPy supports multiple methods that align with various business data scenarios. The array() function converts existing data structures into NumPy arrays, while specialized functions like zeros(), ones(), and empty() create arrays with predefined values. The arange() and linspace() functions generate sequential values, useful for creating time series indices or customer ID sequences. Random number generation through numpy.random supports simulation and statistical analysis common in business forecasting and risk assessment.

Shape manipulation represents a crucial aspect of data processing in business analytics. NumPy arrays can be reshaped, split, and combined efficiently. The reshape() function transforms arrays into different dimensions while maintaining the same data, enabling analysts to restructure data for various analytical purposes. This proves particularly valuable when preparing data for machine learning models or reorganizing sales data across different dimensional views.

Broadcasting in NumPy provides a powerful mechanism for performing operations between arrays of different shapes. This capability simplifies calculations common in business analytics, such as applying percentage adjustments across product lines or computing customer-specific metrics across multiple time periods. Understanding broadcasting rules helps analysts write more efficient and maintainable code.

Mathematical operations in NumPy offer comprehensive support for business calculations. Basic arithmetic operations are vectorized, allowing rapid computation across large datasets. Advanced mathematical functions support financial calculations, statistical analysis, and complex business metrics. The library includes trigonometric functions, exponential and logarithmic operations, and statistical methods essential for business modeling and analysis.

Array indexing and slicing in NumPy provide flexible ways to access and modify data. Boolean indexing enables powerful filtering operations based on complex conditions, essential for identifying specific business scenarios or customer segments. Advanced indexing supports sophisticated data selection patterns that match real-world analytical requirements.

Statistical functions in NumPy support essential business analytics tasks. Methods for computing means, medians, standard deviations, and correlations operate efficiently on large datasets. These functions form the foundation for more complex analytical procedures like customer behavior analysis, product performance evaluation, and market trend assessment.

Linear algebra operations in NumPy enable sophisticated business modeling and analysis. Matrix operations support portfolio optimization, customer similarity calculations, and recommendation systems. The library provides efficient implementations of dot products, matrix decomposition, and eigenvalue calculations crucial for advanced business analytics applications.

File input and output operations in NumPy support efficient data storage and retrieval. The save() and load() functions enable quick persistence of numerical data, while specialized functions handle various file formats. This capability proves valuable when working with large datasets or implementing data caching strategies.

Memory management becomes crucial when working with large business datasets. NumPy provides tools to control memory usage through data type specification and array creation options. Understanding memory layout and optimization techniques helps analysts build scalable solutions that handle growing data volumes efficiently.

Integration with Pandas enhances both libraries' capabilities. NumPy arrays form the underlying data structure for Pandas Series and DataFrames, enabling seamless interaction between numerical computations and data manipulation tasks. This integration supports comprehensive data processing workflows common in business analytics.

Performance optimization in NumPy relies on understanding vectorization principles. Vectorized operations eliminate explicit loops, leveraging efficient C-level implementations. This approach significantly improves processing speed for large datasets common in business applications.

Error handling in NumPy requires attention to numerical computation issues. Understanding concepts like floating-point precision, overflow, and underflow helps analysts build robust analytical solutions. The library provides tools to handle these situations appropriately, ensuring reliable results.

Structured arrays in NumPy support complex data types that match business data structures. This capability enables efficient storage and processing of heterogeneous data while maintaining NumPy's performance advantages. Structured arrays prove particularly valuable when working with fixed-format data common in business systems.

Random number generation capabilities in NumPy support various business applications, from simulation studies to sampling procedures. The library provides multiple probability distributions and random sampling methods essential for risk analysis, customer behavior modeling, and market research applications.

Array operations in NumPy extend beyond basic mathematical functions to include set operations, sorting, and searching capabilities. These features support various business analysis tasks, from customer segmentation to product categorization and market basket analysis.

As we progress through more advanced topics in this book, these NumPy fundamentals will serve as essential tools for efficient data processing and numerical computation in business analytics contexts. The library's combination of performance, flexibility, and comprehensive functionality makes it an indispensable component of modern business analytics solutions.

6. Reading and Writing Data: Multiple File Formats

Reading and writing data efficiently across multiple file formats represents a fundamental skill in business analytics, as organizations often deal with data stored in various formats and sources. This chapter explores the comprehensive approaches to handling different file formats in Python, ensuring analysts can seamlessly work with diverse data sources.

CSV (Comma Separated Values) files remain one of the most common formats for business data exchange. Pandas provides robust functionality for handling CSV files through read_csv() and to_csv() functions. These functions offer extensive customization options to handle various CSV variants. Parameters like delimiter, encoding, and header options allow analysts to properly interpret files with different structures. When dealing with large CSV files, chunking becomes essential. The chunksize parameter enables processing of large files in manageable pieces, preventing memory overload while maintaining processing efficiency.

Excel files present their own unique challenges and opportunities. The read_excel() function supports both older .xls and modern .xlsx formats. Multiple worksheets can be read selectively or all at once, and specific ranges can be targeted for import. When writing to Excel, to_excel() offers formatting options to create professional-looking outputs. The ExcelWriter class provides additional control over Excel file creation, allowing multiple DataFrames to be written to different worksheets while maintaining formatting and structure.

JSON (JavaScript Object Notation) has become increasingly important for data exchange, particularly in web-based applications and APIs. Pandas read_json() handles various JSON structures, including records, split, and index formats. The function can process nested JSON structures, though complex hierarchies might require additional transformation. When writing JSON, to_json() supports different orientations to match specific application requirements. Understanding JSON normalization helps when dealing with nested structures common in API responses.

SQL databases represent a crucial data source in business environments. The read_sql() function provides a direct interface to various database systems through SQLAlchemy. This allows analysts to execute SQL queries and import results directly into DataFrames. Connection management becomes important when dealing with databases, ensuring efficient resource utilization. The to_sql() function enables writing DataFrames back to databases, supporting both creation of new tables and appending to existing ones.

XML files, though less common than other formats, still play a role in certain business systems, particularly legacy applications. The read_xml() function handles XML data, though complex XML structures might require additional processing using libraries like lxml. Understanding XML namespaces and hierarchy becomes important when dealing with complex business documents like electronic invoices or industry-specific formats.

Parquet files have gained popularity for their efficient storage and quick read capabilities, particularly in big data environments. The read_parquet() function provides access to this columnar storage format, offering significant performance advantages for large datasets. Parquet files support compression and encoding options that can dramatically reduce storage requirements while maintaining quick access to data.

HDF5 (Hierarchical Data Format) provides another option for efficient storage of large datasets. The read_hdf() function supports access to these binary format files, which can store multiple DataFrames in a single file. HDF5 offers advantages in terms of read performance and storage efficiency, particularly for time series data common in business analytics.

Text files with various formats often require custom parsing approaches. The read_fwf() function handles fixed-width format files common in legacy systems. For more complex formats, combining read_csv() with custom parsing logic provides flexibility to handle virtually any text-based format.

Web data scraping, while not strictly a file format, represents another important data source. Pandas read_html() function extracts tables from HTML pages, though web scraping often requires additional libraries like BeautifulSoup or Selenium for more complex scenarios. Understanding HTML structure and web protocols helps in building robust scraping solutions.

Compression handling becomes important when dealing with large files. Most Pandas reading functions support compressed files directly, handling formats like gzip, bzip2, and zip. This capability helps manage storage requirements while maintaining easy access to historical data.

Error handling during file operations requires careful consideration. Implementing proper exception handling ensures robust data loading processes. Common issues include encoding problems, malformed data, and network connectivity issues when accessing remote sources.

Performance optimization for file operations often involves choosing appropriate parameters and formats. Understanding options like data types, chunking, and compression can significantly impact loading and saving times. For frequently accessed data, considering memory-mapped files or caching strategies can improve performance.

Data validation during file operations helps ensure data quality. Implementing checks during reading and writing operations catches issues early in the data pipeline. This might include format validation, data type verification, and business rule checking.

When dealing with multiple file formats in a single application, developing consistent interfaces helps manage complexity. Creating wrapper functions that handle different formats while presenting a uniform interface to the application simplifies code maintenance and reduces errors.

Version compatibility requires attention, particularly when dealing with older file formats or when sharing files across different systems. Understanding format specifications and maintaining compatibility information helps prevent issues when exchanging data with other systems or organizations.

File naming and organization strategies become important when managing many data files. Implementing consistent naming conventions and directory structures helps maintain organized data assets. This becomes particularly important in automated processes where files are created or processed programmatically.

Security considerations cannot be ignored when handling file operations. Implementing proper access controls and data encryption where necessary protects sensitive business information. Understanding and following organizational data handling policies ensures compliance with business requirements.

The ability to efficiently read and write different file formats enables analysts to work with diverse data sources and integrate them into comprehensive analytical solutions. As data sources continue to evolve, maintaining flexibility in file handling capabilities remains crucial for effective business analytics.

7. Basic Data Cleaning Operations

Basic data cleaning operations form the foundation of any successful data analysis project in business settings. Without clean, properly formatted data, even the most sophisticated analysis techniques can lead to incorrect conclusions. This chapter explores fundamental data cleaning operations that business analysts encounter in their daily work with Python.

Data cleaning begins with initial data inspection. The first step involves understanding the structure and content of your dataset. Pandas provides several useful functions for this purpose. The info() method gives a quick overview of your DataFrame, showing data types, non null counts, and memory usage. The describe() method provides basic statistical information about numerical columns, while value_counts() helps understand the distribution of categorical data. These preliminary inspections often reveal the most obvious data quality issues that need addressing.

Duplicate records represent a common data quality issue that can significantly impact analysis results. In business datasets, duplicates might arise from multiple data entry points, system glitches, or merge operations. Pandas provides straightforward methods to identify and handle duplicates. The duplicated() method identifies duplicate rows, while drop_duplicates() removes them. When dealing with duplicates, it's crucial to understand which columns should be considered for determining uniqueness. In customer data, for example, multiple transactions from the same customer shouldn't be considered duplicates, but multiple identical transaction records likely should be.

Standardization of data format and values represents another critical aspect of data cleaning. Inconsistent formatting often occurs in text fields, such as company names, addresses, or product descriptions. Simple string operations can help standardize these values. For example, using str.lower() or str.upper() ensures consistent case formatting. The str.strip() method removes unwanted whitespace, while str.replace() can handle specific character replacements. More complex standardization might involve regular expressions, particularly useful for formatting phone numbers, postal codes, or other structured text data.

Outlier detection and handling requires careful consideration in business contexts. While statistical methods like z-scores or interquartile ranges can identify numerical outliers, business knowledge remains crucial in determining appropriate actions. Some outliers might represent genuine but unusual business events, while others might indicate data errors. Visualization tools like box plots or scatter plots help in identifying outliers visually. Once identified, outliers can be removed, capped at certain values, or flagged for further investigation depending on the business context.

Data type conversion often becomes necessary when data is imported from various sources. Numbers stored as strings, datetime information in incorrect formats, or categorical data stored as numerical values are common issues. Pandas provides various methods for type conversion, including astype() for basic conversions and to_datetime() for handling date and time data. When performing conversions, error handling becomes important, as failed conversions can indicate data quality issues that need investigation.

Value normalization helps ensure consistency across numerical data. This might involve scaling values to a common range, converting between different units of measurement, or standardizing currency amounts. For example, financial data might mix different currencies or use various scales (thousands vs. millions). Implementing consistent normalization rules ensures meaningful comparisons and aggregations.

Column naming and organization plays a crucial role in maintaining clean datasets. Consistent naming conventions make data more understandable and easier to work with. Common operations include renaming columns to follow conventions, reordering columns for logical organization, and dropping unnecessary columns. The rename() method allows systematic column renaming, while drop() removes unneeded columns.

Data validation rules help maintain data quality during cleaning operations. These rules might check for valid value ranges, ensure proper relationships between fields, or verify business logic constraints. For example, order dates should not be later than shipping dates, or product prices should fall within expected ranges. Implementing these checks during cleaning helps identify potential issues early in the analysis process.

Handling special characters and encoding issues often arises when working with international data or data from various sources. Understanding character encodings and implementing proper handling prevents garbled text or data corruption. The encode() and decode() string methods help manage these situations, while specifying correct encodings during file reading prevents issues from arising.

Creating audit trails during cleaning operations helps maintain transparency and reproducibility. Logging the number of records affected by each cleaning operation, keeping track of removed duplicates, and documenting handling of special cases provides valuable information for validating results and troubleshooting issues.

Dealing with inconsistent categories represents another common challenge. Business data often contains variations in category names due to typos, different naming conventions, or changes over time. Creating mapping dictionaries to standardize categories, using fuzzy matching for similar values, and maintaining category hierarchies helps manage these situations.

Data cleaning workflows often need to be repeatable and scalable. Creating functions or classes to encapsulate cleaning operations makes the process more maintainable and reusable. This modular approach allows cleaning operations to be applied consistently across different datasets or time periods.

Performance considerations become important when cleaning large datasets. Vectorized operations in Pandas generally perform better than iterative approaches. Understanding when to use apply() versus vectorized operations, and when to leverage other optimization techniques helps maintain efficient cleaning processes.

Documentation of cleaning decisions and processes proves invaluable for future reference. Recording the rationale behind cleaning decisions, maintaining lists of standard cleaning rules, and documenting special cases helps ensure consistency and knowledge transfer within analytics teams.

The impact of data cleaning decisions on subsequent analysis should always be considered. Aggressive cleaning might remove important business insights, while insufficient cleaning could lead to incorrect conclusions. Finding the right balance requires both technical understanding and business context.

Regular review and updating of cleaning procedures ensures they remain relevant as business requirements evolve. What constitutes "clean" data might change over time as business rules update or new data quality issues emerge. Maintaining flexible and adaptable cleaning processes helps handle these changes effectively.

8. Handling Missing Data in Business Datasets

Handling missing data represents one of the most critical challenges in business data analysis. Missing values can significantly impact analysis results and lead to incorrect business decisions if not handled appropriately. Understanding the nature of missing data and implementing suitable strategies for handling it forms an essential skill for business analysts working with Python.

Missing data in business contexts can arise from various sources. Data entry errors, system malfunctions, incomplete form submissions, or intentionally skipped fields all contribute to missing values. Understanding why data is missing helps determine the most appropriate handling strategy. Missing data typically falls into three categories: Missing Completely at Random (MCAR), Missing at Random (MAR), and Missing Not at Random (MNAR). Each type requires different handling approaches based on the underlying mechanisms causing the missing values.

The first step in handling missing data involves detecting and quantifying the extent of missing values. Pandas provides several tools for this purpose. The isnull() and isna() methods identify missing values, while info() provides an overview of non null counts across columns. Computing the percentage of missing values per column helps prioritize handling efforts. Visualization techniques, such as heatmaps of missing value patterns, can reveal relationships between missing values across different variables.

Simple missing value detection sometimes fails to capture all forms of missing data. Business datasets often use special codes or values to represent missing information, such as -999, 'N/A', or empty strings. Standardizing these representations to proper missing value formats (None or NaN) ensures consistent handling throughout the analysis process. This standardization might involve replacing specific values or implementing custom missing value detection logic based on business rules.

Different business contexts require different strategies for handling missing values. In customer demographic data, missing values might be filled with the mode or median of the population. In financial time series, interpolation between existing values might make more sense. Sales data might require more sophisticated imputation methods based on seasonal patterns or related product information. The choice of strategy depends on the nature of the data and the requirements of subsequent analysis.

Simple imputation methods include filling with statistical measures like mean, median, or mode. While straightforward to implement using fillna(), these methods can distort relationships in the data and underestimate variability. More sophisticated approaches might involve forward or backward filling (particularly useful for time series data), or using the nearest neighbor values. The bfill() and ffill() methods in Pandas facilitate these operations.

Multiple imputation represents a more advanced approach to handling missing values. This technique creates multiple complete datasets with different imputed values, allowing for uncertainty in the imputation process. Libraries like sklearn.impute provide implementations of various multiple imputation methods. While more complex to implement, multiple imputation often provides more reliable results for subsequent analysis.

Machine learning based imputation offers another sophisticated approach. Methods like k-nearest neighbors imputation or regression based imputation can capture complex relationships in the data to predict missing values. These methods prove particularly valuable when missing values show clear patterns or relationships with other variables in the dataset.

Sometimes, removing records or variables with missing values becomes necessary. The dropna() method facilitates this process, allowing removal based on various criteria. However, removal decisions should consider the potential impact on analysis results. Removing too many records might introduce bias or reduce statistical power, while removing important variables might omit crucial business information.

When dealing with time series data, special consideration must be given to missing values. Business time series often contain gaps due to non business days, system downtimes, or reporting issues. Resampling techniques, combined with appropriate imputation methods, help handle these situations. Rolling windows or exponential smoothing might provide appropriate values for missing time points.

Missing values in categorical variables present unique challenges. Simple statistical imputation might not make sense for categories. Creating a new "Unknown" or "Missing" category might better represent the reality of the data, particularly in customer segmentation or product classification scenarios. However, this approach requires careful consideration of how these new categories will impact subsequent analysis.

Documentation of missing value handling decisions proves crucial for reproducibility and validation. Recording the rationale behind chosen imputation methods, maintaining logs of the number of values imputed, and tracking the impact on key business metrics helps ensure transparency and enables future refinement of handling strategies.

Regular monitoring of missing data patterns helps identify potential systemic issues in data collection or processing. Sudden changes in missing value patterns might indicate problems with data collection systems or changes in business processes that need addressing. Implementing automated monitoring systems helps catch these issues early.

Performance considerations become important when handling missing values in large datasets. Vectorized operations generally perform better than iterative approaches. Understanding when to use different Pandas methods and how to optimize missing value handling operations helps maintain efficient processing pipelines.

The impact of missing value handling on subsequent analysis requires careful evaluation. Different imputation methods might lead to different analysis results. Sensitivity analysis, comparing results across different imputation strategies, helps understand the robustness of conclusions to missing value handling choices.

Integration with broader data quality frameworks ensures consistent handling of missing values across different analyses and teams. Establishing standard procedures for different types of missing data, maintaining documentation of handling rules, and regularly reviewing and updating these procedures helps maintain data quality standards.

Missing value handling strategies often need to adapt to changing business requirements and data characteristics. What works for current data might need adjustment as business processes evolve or new data sources are incorporated. Maintaining flexible and adaptable handling procedures helps manage these changes effectively.

9. Data Validation Fundamentals

Data validation represents a cornerstone of reliable business analytics, serving as the first line of defense against data quality issues that could compromise analysis results. Implementing robust validation procedures ensures that data meets expected standards and business rules before proceeding with analysis, saving countless hours of troubleshooting and preventing potentially costly decisions based on faulty data.

Data validation begins with understanding the expected characteristics and constraints of business data. This includes defining acceptable ranges for numerical values, valid formats for dates and identifiers, logical relationships between fields, and business specific rules that data must satisfy. For example, sales amounts should never be negative, customer ages should fall within reasonable ranges, and transaction dates shouldn't occur in the future.

Python provides several approaches to implementing data validation checks. The most straightforward method involves using basic comparison operations and boolean masks in Pandas. These allow analysts to identify records that violate specific conditions. For example, checking for values outside acceptable ranges can be accomplished using simple comparison operators, while more complex validation rules might require combining multiple conditions using logical operators.

Custom validation functions enable more sophisticated checks that incorporate business logic. These functions can encapsulate complex validation rules and return boolean indicators of validity. By applying these functions to Pandas DataFrames using apply() or transform() methods, analysts can systematically validate large datasets against multiple criteria simultaneously.

Regular expressions prove invaluable for validating text data formats. Whether checking email addresses, phone numbers, or product codes, Python's re module provides powerful pattern matching capabilities. Combined with Pandas string methods, regular expressions enable efficient validation of text fields across large datasets, ensuring consistency in data formats.

Schema validation represents a more structured approach to data validation. Libraries like pandera allow definition of explicit schemas that specify expected data types, value ranges, and relationships between fields. These schemas serve both as documentation of data requirements and as automated validation tools, catching violations before they impact analysis.

Cross field validation ensures logical consistency between related data elements. For example, verifying that order dates precede shipping dates, or that subtotals sum correctly to totals. These checks often require combining information from multiple columns and applying business specific logic to identify inconsistencies.

Temporal validation becomes particularly important when dealing with time series data. This includes checking for proper chronological ordering, identifying gaps in time series, and validating that time dependent relationships make sense. For instance, ensuring that cumulative values increase over time or that seasonal patterns align with business cycles.

Statistical validation methods help identify potential anomalies that might not violate explicit business rules but could indicate data quality issues. This includes checking for outliers using statistical measures, verifying distributional assumptions, and identifying unusual patterns that warrant further investigation.

Validation against reference data represents another crucial aspect of data quality assurance. This might involve checking that customer IDs exist in a master customer database, that product codes match an approved list, or that geographical data aligns with known locations. Such validation often requires joining or merging operations to compare data against reference sources.

Automated validation workflows improve efficiency and consistency in data validation processes. By creating reusable validation functions and combining them into automated pipelines, analysts can systematically check new data against established criteria. This automation reduces manual effort and ensures consistent application of validation rules.

Error handling and reporting form essential components of validation frameworks. When validation checks fail, clear error messages should indicate the nature and location of violations. Generating detailed validation reports helps track data quality issues over time and communicate problems to data providers or stakeholders.

Performance considerations become important when validating large datasets. Vectorized operations generally perform better than iterative approaches, and careful attention to validation check ordering can improve efficiency. Some validation checks might be parallelizable, allowing for faster processing of large datasets.

Validation rules often need to evolve with changing business requirements and data characteristics. Maintaining validation logic in a centralized, version controlled location facilitates updates and ensures consistency across different analyses. Regular review and updating of validation rules helps keep them aligned with current business needs.

Integration with data ingestion processes ensures that validation occurs at the earliest possible stage. By validating data as it enters analysis systems, problems can be caught and addressed before they impact downstream processes. This might involve implementing validation checks within ETL pipelines or data loading scripts.

Documentation of validation rules and procedures proves crucial for maintaining data quality standards across teams and over time. This includes documenting the rationale behind validation rules, maintaining clear descriptions of validation checks, and recording any exceptions or special cases that need consideration.

Balancing validation stringency with practical requirements represents an ongoing challenge. While strict validation helps maintain data quality, overly rigid rules might reject valid but unusual data. Finding the right balance requires understanding both technical constraints and business needs.

Exception handling procedures need clear definition for cases where data fails validation but must still be processed. This might involve implementing warning systems for minor violations while still rejecting critical errors, or maintaining separate workflows for handling exceptional cases.

Periodic review of validation results helps identify systematic issues in data quality. Tracking validation failure rates over time can reveal deteriorating data quality or highlight areas needing attention in data collection or processing systems. Regular reviews also help ensure validation rules remain relevant and effective.

The impact of validation procedures on business processes requires careful consideration. While thorough validation helps prevent data quality issues, it can also introduce delays in data processing. Balancing thoroughness with timeliness often requires careful optimization of validation procedures.

10. Building Data Quality Frameworks

Building data quality frameworks represents a systematic approach to ensuring and maintaining data integrity across an organization's analytics processes. While individual validation checks form the foundation of data quality, a comprehensive framework provides structure, consistency, and scalability to data quality efforts.

A robust data quality framework begins with clear definitions of data quality dimensions. These typically include accuracy, completeness, consistency, timeliness, validity, and uniqueness. Each dimension requires specific metrics and assessment methods. For accuracy, this might involve comparison against source systems or verification against physical records. Completeness checks examine both record level and field level missing data patterns. Consistency ensures data adheres to defined rules and relationships across different datasets.

Python offers several approaches to implementing these frameworks. Custom classes can encapsulate quality checks and reporting mechanisms, providing a reusable structure for different datasets. These classes typically include methods for running validation checks, aggregating results, and generating reports. By standardizing the interface for quality checks, organizations can more easily maintain and extend their quality control processes.

The framework should incorporate different levels of validation severity. Critical checks might prevent data from entering analysis pipelines if failed, while warning level checks might flag potential issues for review without blocking processing. This tiered approach allows organizations to balance data quality requirements with operational needs.

Configuration management plays a crucial role in quality frameworks. Validation rules, acceptable thresholds, and quality metrics often need adjustment based on changing business requirements or data characteristics. Storing these configurations in easily maintainable formats like YAML or JSON files allows for flexible updates without modifying code.

Logging and monitoring capabilities form essential components of quality frameworks. Detailed logs of validation results help track data quality trends over time and provide audit trails for compliance purposes. Monitoring systems can alert relevant stakeholders when quality metrics fall below acceptable thresholds or when unusual patterns emerge.

Integration with existing data pipelines requires careful consideration. Quality frameworks should provide interfaces that allow seamless incorporation into ETL processes, analytical workflows, and reporting systems. This might involve creating wrapper functions or adapters that standardize how different systems interact with quality checks.

Performance optimization becomes crucial as data volumes grow. Quality frameworks should implement efficient validation strategies, possibly including parallel processing for large datasets. Caching mechanisms can help avoid redundant calculations, while intelligent check ordering can minimize computational overhead.

Reporting capabilities need to serve different stakeholder needs. Technical users might require detailed validation results and error messages, while business users might need high level quality metrics and trend analysis. The framework should support generating appropriate reports for different audiences.

Version control and documentation ensure framework maintainability. Quality rules often evolve over time, and maintaining a clear history of changes helps understand how data quality requirements have shifted. Documentation should cover both technical implementation details and business rationale for quality rules.

Error handling and recovery procedures need careful design. The framework should gracefully handle various failure scenarios, from individual validation check failures to system level issues. Clear protocols for error resolution and data correction help maintain smooth operations.

Scalability considerations extend beyond just handling large datasets. The framework should accommodate new data sources, additional quality checks, and evolving business requirements without requiring significant restructuring. Modular design patterns help achieve this flexibility.

Training and knowledge transfer mechanisms ensure consistent framework usage across teams. This includes documentation of best practices, example implementations, and common troubleshooting approaches. Regular training sessions help maintain high standards of data quality management.

Compliance and governance requirements often influence framework design. Many industries have specific regulations regarding data quality and validation. The framework should support generating evidence of compliance and maintaining audit trails of quality checks.

Integration with data profiling tools can enhance framework effectiveness. Automated profiling helps identify potential quality issues and suggest appropriate validation rules. This can significantly speed up the process of implementing quality checks for new datasets.

The framework should support both automated and manual quality checks. While automation improves efficiency, some quality aspects might require human judgment. The framework should facilitate combining automated validation with manual review processes.

Feedback loops help improve framework effectiveness over time. Regular review of validation results, error patterns, and user feedback helps identify areas for improvement. This might lead to refinement of validation rules, adjustment of thresholds, or addition of new quality checks.

Cost benefit analysis helps optimize framework implementation. While comprehensive quality checks provide better data reliability, they also consume computational resources and potentially introduce processing delays. The framework should help balance these tradeoffs based on business requirements.

Security considerations include protecting sensitive validation rules and quality metrics. Access controls ensure that only authorized users can modify quality checks or view detailed validation results. The framework should integrate with organizational security policies and procedures.

Regular framework evaluation ensures continued effectiveness. This includes reviewing whether quality metrics align with business needs, assessing framework performance and scalability, and identifying opportunities for improvement. Periodic reviews help maintain framework relevance and effectiveness.

11. String Operations and Text Cleaning

String operations and text cleaning represent fundamental skills in data wrangling, particularly when dealing with business data that often contains unstructured or semi-structured text. Text data appears in various forms across business operations, from customer feedback and product descriptions to transaction notes and communication logs. Effective text processing ensures this valuable information can be properly analyzed and utilized for business insights.

Python provides powerful string manipulation capabilities through both built-in string methods and specialized libraries. The string methods in Python offer fundamental operations like splitting, joining, case conversion, and pattern matching. These basic operations form the foundation of text cleaning workflows. For instance, standardizing case across text fields ensures consistent analysis, while splitting operations help parse structured text into meaningful components.

Regular expressions (regex) play a crucial role in advanced text processing. Python's re module provides comprehensive regex functionality for pattern matching and text extraction. Business analysts frequently encounter scenarios where they need to extract specific patterns like email addresses, phone numbers, or product codes from text fields. Regular expressions offer precise control over these extraction tasks, though they require careful construction to handle variations in text patterns.

Text standardization represents a common challenge in business data. Customer names, addresses, and product descriptions often contain variations in formatting, spelling, or abbreviation. Creating standardization rules helps ensure consistency across datasets. This might involve removing special characters, standardizing abbreviations, or applying specific formatting rules based on business requirements.

Whitespace handling requires particular attention in text cleaning. Excess spaces, tabs, or line breaks can cause issues in data processing and analysis. Python's strip, lstrip, and rstrip methods help remove unwanted whitespace, while more complex cases might require custom functions to handle specific formatting requirements. Business documents often contain formatting artifacts when converted between systems, making whitespace cleanup an essential step in data preparation.

Character encoding issues frequently arise when working with text data from multiple sources. Python 3's native Unicode support helps manage different character encodings, but proper handling requires understanding the source data's encoding and implementing appropriate conversion methods. International business data often contains special characters or non-Latin alphabets that need careful handling to preserve information integrity.

Text normalization encompasses various techniques for standardizing text content. This includes removing accents, converting special characters to standard forms, and handling language-specific variations. Business data often contains product names or customer information in multiple languages, requiring consistent normalization approaches to enable accurate analysis.

Spell checking and correction capabilities help clean messy text data. While perfect spelling correction remains challenging, identifying and correcting common misspellings improves data quality. Python libraries like pyspellchecker provide functionality for basic spell checking, though business-specific terms often require custom dictionaries or correction rules.

String concatenation and formatting operations help combine or restructure text data. Business reports often require specific text formatting, and Python's string formatting methods provide flexible tools for creating standardized output. This includes both basic string concatenation and more complex template-based formatting approaches.

Text parsing represents another crucial aspect of string operations. Breaking down complex text fields into structured components requires careful parsing logic. This might involve extracting dates from text descriptions, separating address components, or identifying product attributes from descriptions. Custom parsing functions often combine multiple string operations to handle specific business data formats.

Error handling in text processing requires robust approaches. Invalid characters, unexpected formats, or encoding issues can disrupt processing workflows. Implementing proper error handling ensures text cleaning operations can handle problematic data without failing. This includes both detecting issues and implementing appropriate fallback behaviors.

Performance considerations become important when processing large volumes of text data. String operations can be computationally expensive, particularly when applying complex regular expressions or multiple transformations. Optimizing text processing workflows might involve using more efficient methods, implementing caching strategies, or processing text in batches.

Documentation of text cleaning rules ensures consistency and maintainability. Business rules for text standardization often evolve over time, and clear documentation helps teams understand and apply these rules consistently. This includes documenting both the technical implementation and the business rationale behind specific cleaning approaches.

Text data quality assessment requires specific approaches. Beyond basic validation checks, text fields might need evaluation for completeness, consistency, and meaningfulness. Developing appropriate quality metrics for text data helps monitor the effectiveness of cleaning operations and identify areas needing improvement.

Integration with natural language processing (NLP) workflows often follows text cleaning. Clean, standardized text provides a better foundation for more advanced NLP tasks like sentiment analysis or topic modeling. Understanding how cleaned text will be used in subsequent analysis helps inform appropriate cleaning strategies.

Version control for text cleaning rules helps manage evolving requirements. As business needs change or new text patterns emerge, cleaning rules often need updates. Maintaining version control ensures changes can be tracked and previous versions can be referenced if needed.

Testing text cleaning operations requires comprehensive test cases. Different text patterns, special cases, and error conditions need testing to ensure robust operation. Creating test suites that cover various scenarios helps maintain cleaning quality as implementations evolve.

The relationship between text cleaning and business rules requires careful consideration. Some apparent inconsistencies in text might actually represent meaningful business variations. Understanding when to standardize and when to preserve variations requires close collaboration with business stakeholders.

Automated text cleaning workflows need to balance thoroughness with processing efficiency. While comprehensive cleaning improves data quality, excessive processing can impact system performance. Finding appropriate trade-offs between cleaning depth and processing requirements helps create practical solutions.

Finally, maintaining text cleaning operations requires ongoing attention. New data sources, changing business requirements, or emerging text patterns might necessitate updates to cleaning procedures. Regular review and refinement of text cleaning workflows helps ensure continued effectiveness in supporting business analytics needs.

12. Date and Time Data Processing

Date and time data processing represents a critical component of business data analysis, as temporal information underlies virtually every business operation, from transaction timestamps to schedule management. Understanding how to effectively handle date and time data in Python enables analysts to perform accurate time-based analysis and create reliable business insights.

Python's datetime module provides the foundation for date and time manipulation. This built-in module offers classes for representing dates, times, and timestamps, along with methods for performing calculations and conversions. The datetime, date, and time classes handle different aspects of temporal data, while timedelta enables precise time period calculations essential for business analytics.

Parsing dates from various formats presents a common challenge in business data. Different systems, regions, and data sources often use different date formats, requiring flexible parsing approaches. The datetime.strptime method provides powerful parsing capabilities, while pandas' to_datetime function offers additional flexibility for handling diverse date formats commonly encountered in business data.

Time zone handling requires particular attention in global business operations. Python's pytz library, along with datetime's tzinfo functionality, enables proper management of time zone conversions and calculations. Business data often spans multiple time zones, and proper handling ensures accurate temporal analysis across international operations.

Date arithmetic forms a crucial part of business analysis. Calculating time differences, adding or subtracting time periods, and determining business days all require precise date manipulation. The timedelta class enables these calculations, while business day calculations might require additional libraries like pandas' business day functionality to account for holidays and working days.

Timestamp precision varies across business systems, requiring careful handling during data integration. Some systems might record microsecond-level precision, while others might round to the nearest second or minute. Understanding and standardizing timestamp precision ensures consistent analysis across different data sources.

Period calculations represent another essential aspect of date processing. Business metrics often involve specific periods like fiscal quarters, rolling windows, or custom business periods. Python's date handling capabilities enable flexible period definitions and calculations, supporting various business calendar requirements.

Date validation plays a crucial role in ensuring data quality. Beyond basic format validation, business dates must often meet specific criteria like falling within valid ranges or matching expected patterns. Implementing robust date validation helps identify and handle invalid or problematic date data before it affects analysis.

Time series resampling enables analysis at different temporal granularities. Business data might be collected at one time interval but need analysis at another, requiring appropriate resampling methods. Pandas provides powerful resampling capabilities for aggregating or interpolating time series data to meet various analysis requirements.

Date formatting for output and display requires consideration of business and regional standards. Python's strftime method and pandas' date formatting capabilities enable flexible output formatting. Creating standardized date representations ensures consistency in reports and analyses across the organization.

Holiday handling adds complexity to business date calculations. Different regions and organizations observe different holidays, affecting business day calculations and scheduling analysis. Python libraries like pandas provide holiday calendars, while custom holiday definitions enable organization-specific date handling.

Fiscal year calculations often differ from calendar years in business contexts. Python's date handling capabilities enable custom fiscal period calculations, supporting various fiscal calendar definitions and period-based analysis requirements.

Performance optimization becomes important when processing large volumes of date data. Efficient date parsing and calculation methods help maintain system performance. Understanding Python's date handling optimizations and implementing appropriate strategies ensures efficient processing of temporal data.

Date data quality assessment requires specific approaches. Beyond format validation, dates must often meet business logic requirements like proper sequencing or alignment with business events. Developing comprehensive date validation frameworks helps maintain data quality.

Integration with databases requires understanding date type mappings. Different database systems handle dates differently, and proper mapping ensures accurate data transfer. Python's database interfaces provide methods for handling date conversions between systems.

Automated date processing workflows need robust error handling. Invalid dates, unexpected formats, or timezone issues can disrupt processing. Implementing appropriate error handling ensures reliable operation of date-dependent processes.

Historical date handling presents unique challenges. Legacy systems might use different date formats or conventions, requiring special handling. Understanding common historical date formats and implementing appropriate conversion methods ensures accurate processing of historical data.

Future dates and forecasting require careful handling of date ranges. Business planning often involves future dates, and proper date handling ensures accurate projections and scheduling. Python's date capabilities support both historical and future date operations.

Documentation of date handling rules ensures consistency across applications. Date processing often involves complex business rules and conventions that need clear documentation. Maintaining comprehensive documentation helps teams understand and correctly implement date handling requirements.

Version control for date processing logic helps manage evolving requirements. As business needs change or new date handling requirements emerge, maintaining version control ensures changes can be tracked and previous implementations can be referenced if needed.

Testing date processing operations requires comprehensive test cases. Different date patterns, special cases, and edge conditions need testing to ensure robust operation. Creating thorough test suites helps maintain reliability of date-dependent processes.

Finally, maintaining date processing operations requires ongoing attention to changing requirements. New data sources, business rules, or regulatory requirements might necessitate updates to date handling procedures. Regular review and refinement of date processing workflows helps ensure continued effectiveness in supporting business analytics needs.

13. Numerical Data Preprocessing

Numerical data preprocessing forms the backbone of quantitative business analysis, requiring careful attention to ensure data quality and analytical validity. Raw numerical data often contains inconsistencies, outliers, and scale variations that must be addressed before meaningful analysis can proceed. Understanding and implementing proper numerical preprocessing techniques enables analysts to create reliable foundations for business insights.

Data type conversion represents the first critical step in numerical preprocessing. Business data often arrives with numbers stored as strings or in incompatible formats. Python's numeric data types, including integers and floating-point numbers, provide the foundation for proper numerical handling. Converting data to appropriate numeric types ensures calculations proceed accurately and efficiently.

Scale standardization plays a crucial role when working with variables of different magnitudes. Business metrics often span different scales, from percentages to millions of dollars, making direct comparisons challenging. Techniques like min-max scaling and standardization (z-score normalization) enable meaningful comparisons across different numerical features while preserving relative relationships within the data.

Outlier detection and handling requires careful consideration of business context. Statistical methods like z-score analysis and interquartile range calculations help identify potential outliers, but business knowledge must guide their treatment. Some outliers represent legitimate business events that should be preserved, while others might result from data errors requiring correction or removal.

Missing value imputation for numerical data demands sophisticated approaches. Simple techniques like mean or median imputation might suffice for basic cases, but business data often requires more nuanced methods. Multiple imputation, regression-based approaches, or domain-specific rules might better preserve the data's statistical properties and business meaning.

Binning and discretization transform continuous numerical data into categorical ranges when business analysis requires grouped data. Different binning strategies, from equal-width to quantile-based approaches, serve different analytical needs. The choice of binning method can significantly impact subsequent analysis and should align with business objectives.

Normalization techniques become essential when dealing with different units of measurement. Business data often combines metrics in different units, from currencies to physical measurements. Proper normalization ensures meaningful comparisons and analysis across different measurement systems while maintaining relative relationships within the data.

Decimal precision handling requires attention to business requirements and computational limitations. Different business contexts demand different levels of precision, from whole numbers in inventory counts to multiple decimal places in financial calculations. Understanding Python's decimal handling capabilities helps maintain appropriate precision while avoiding computational errors.

Mathematical transformations often improve data characteristics for analysis. Logarithmic transformations can help handle skewed distributions, while power transformations might better reveal relationships in the data. Selecting appropriate transformations requires understanding both statistical properties and business implications.

Currency conversion and standardization presents unique challenges in international business data. Exchange rates, historical rate handling, and currency precision requirements add complexity to numerical preprocessing. Implementing robust currency handling ensures consistent financial analysis across different regions and time periods.

Percentage calculations require careful handling to maintain accuracy. Business metrics often involve percentages, ratios, and proportions that must be calculated and stored appropriately. Understanding percentage arithmetic and proper storage formats helps prevent common calculation errors.

Rounding rules need to align with business requirements and accounting standards. Different contexts require different rounding approaches, from simple decimal truncation to complex rounding rules for financial calculations. Implementing appropriate rounding methods ensures consistency with business standards.

Aggregation methods for numerical data must preserve meaningful business relationships. Different aggregation functions serve different analytical needs, from simple sums and averages to weighted calculations and custom metrics. Selecting appropriate aggregation methods ensures meaningful summary statistics.

Correlation analysis requires properly preprocessed numerical data to yield valid insights. Checking and handling linear dependencies, multicollinearity, and relationship patterns helps identify potential data quality issues and analytical opportunities. Understanding correlation preprocessing requirements improves the reliability of subsequent analyses.

Performance optimization becomes crucial when processing large numerical datasets. Efficient data types, vectorized operations, and appropriate memory management help maintain system performance. Understanding Python's numerical processing capabilities enables efficient handling of large-scale business data.

Validation frameworks for numerical data need to incorporate both statistical and business rules. Range checks, relationship validation, and consistency verification help maintain data quality. Developing comprehensive numerical validation procedures ensures reliable analytical foundations.

Error handling for numerical operations requires robust approaches to handle edge cases. Division by zero, overflow conditions, and precision limitations need appropriate handling. Implementing comprehensive error handling ensures reliable operation of numerical processing workflows.

Documentation of numerical preprocessing decisions ensures reproducibility and transparency. Recording transformation rules, handling decisions, and validation criteria helps teams understand and maintain preprocessing workflows. Maintaining clear documentation supports long-term maintenance of analytical processes.

Version control for numerical preprocessing helps manage evolving requirements and methods. As business needs change or new preprocessing techniques emerge, maintaining version control ensures changes can be tracked and previous implementations can be referenced if needed.

Testing numerical preprocessing requires comprehensive verification of transformation accuracy. Different data patterns, edge cases, and business scenarios need testing to ensure robust operation. Creating thorough test suites helps maintain reliability of numerical preprocessing workflows.

Regular review and refinement of numerical preprocessing methods ensures continued effectiveness in supporting business analytics. As data sources, business requirements, and analytical methods evolve, preprocessing workflows might need updates to maintain their utility and reliability.

14. Categorical Data Handling

Categorical data presents unique challenges in business analytics, requiring specific handling techniques to transform qualitative information into formats suitable for analysis. Unlike numerical data, categorical variables represent discrete groups or labels that often carry rich business meaning but need careful processing to yield quantitative insights.

Understanding categorical data types forms the foundation of effective handling. Nominal categories, such as product names or customer segments, have no inherent order, while ordinal categories, like customer satisfaction ratings or size classifications, maintain meaningful sequences. Recognizing these distinctions guides appropriate processing strategies and analytical approaches.

Encoding categorical variables transforms text based categories into numerical formats suitable for analysis. One hot encoding creates binary columns for each category, particularly useful when categories have no ordinal relationship. Label encoding assigns numerical values to categories, more appropriate for ordinal data where order matters. Understanding when to apply each encoding method ensures meaningful analytical results.

Category consolidation often becomes necessary when dealing with business data containing too many unique categories. Customer feedback might include hundreds of unique responses that need grouping into manageable categories. Sales data might contain numerous product variants that benefit from hierarchical categorization. Developing systematic approaches to category consolidation helps maintain analytical tractability while preserving business meaning.

Handling missing values in categorical data requires different strategies than numerical missing value treatment. Business context often determines whether missing categories represent meaningful information or data collection issues. Creating appropriate missing value categories, implementing default classifications, or developing imputation strategies based on business rules helps maintain data completeness.

Category validation ensures consistency across datasets and over time. Business data often contains spelling variations, case differences, or alternative representations of the same categories. Implementing standardization rules, maintaining category dictionaries, and developing validation procedures helps ensure consistent categorical data handling.

Hierarchical categories require special attention in business analytics. Product classifications might include multiple levels, from broad categories to specific variants. Geographic data often contains nested relationships between regions, countries, and cities. Implementing proper handling of hierarchical relationships enables multilevel analysis while maintaining data integrity.

Feature creation from categorical data often yields valuable analytical insights. Combining categories, creating interaction terms, or developing derived features based on category characteristics can reveal patterns not apparent in the original data. Understanding feature engineering techniques for categorical data expands analytical possibilities.

Frequency based processing helps handle rare categories and assess category distributions. Some business categories might occur too infrequently for meaningful analysis, requiring special handling or consolidation. Understanding category frequencies helps guide processing decisions and identifies potential data quality issues.

Time varying categories present unique challenges in longitudinal business analysis. Product categories might change over time, customer segments might evolve, or classification systems might be updated. Developing strategies to handle temporal category changes ensures consistent analysis across time periods.

Binary category creation often simplifies analysis while preserving essential business information. Complex categorical variables might be transformed into series of binary flags representing key characteristics. Understanding when and how to create binary categories helps balance analytical simplicity with information preservation.

Category mapping between systems requires careful attention to maintain consistency. Different business systems might use different category schemes for the same concepts. Developing robust mapping procedures and maintaining mapping dictionaries ensures consistent category handling across data sources.

Categorical data validation frameworks need to incorporate business rules and domain knowledge. Category relationships, valid combinations, and temporal constraints often reflect business realities that must be preserved. Implementing comprehensive validation procedures helps maintain categorical data quality.

Performance optimization for categorical data processing becomes crucial with large datasets. Efficient storage formats, appropriate data structures, and optimized processing methods help maintain system performance. Understanding Python's categorical data capabilities enables efficient handling of large scale business data.

Documentation of categorical processing decisions ensures reproducibility and knowledge transfer. Recording category definitions, consolidation rules, and handling procedures helps teams maintain consistent approaches. Clear documentation supports long term maintenance of categorical data processing.

Testing categorical data handling requires verification across different scenarios. Various category combinations, edge cases, and business situations need testing to ensure robust operation. Developing comprehensive test procedures helps maintain reliability of categorical data processing.

Visualization of categorical data helps verify processing results and identify patterns. Category distributions, relationship diagrams, and temporal changes often reveal insights about data quality and processing effectiveness. Incorporating visualization into categorical data handling workflows supports quality assurance.

Integration with numerical analysis requires careful handling of categorical features. Many analytical techniques combine categorical and numerical data, requiring appropriate preprocessing of both types. Understanding the interaction between categorical and numerical processing ensures effective integrated analysis.

Regular review of categorical handling procedures ensures continued alignment with business needs. As business categories evolve, new data sources emerge, or analytical requirements change, processing approaches might need updates. Maintaining current and effective categorical data handling supports ongoing business analytics.

Version control for categorical processing helps manage evolving category schemes and handling methods. As business categories change or new processing techniques emerge, maintaining version control ensures changes can be tracked and previous implementations can be referenced when needed. This systematic approach to categorical data handling provides a foundation for reliable business analytics while maintaining flexibility for evolving business needs.

15. Advanced Data Transformation Techniques

Advanced data transformation techniques represent a crucial skillset for business analysts working with complex datasets. These techniques go beyond basic data cleaning and manipulation, enabling sophisticated analysis and insight generation from raw business data.

Data normalization and standardization form the foundation of advanced transformations. While simple scaling might suffice for basic analysis, business data often requires more nuanced approaches. Feature scaling must consider business context, outlier sensitivity, and downstream analytical requirements. Techniques like robust scaling prove valuable when dealing with financial data containing legitimate but extreme values.

Window functions enable sophisticated time based and sequential analysis. Rolling calculations, cumulative metrics, and period over period comparisons provide essential business insights. Understanding window function parameters and boundary handling ensures accurate analysis of trends, patterns, and business performance over time.

Custom transformations based on business rules require careful implementation. Complex business logic often involves multiple conditions, hierarchical rules, and exception handling. Developing systematic approaches to implementing business rules ensures consistent data transformation while maintaining transparency and maintainability.

Conditional transformations enable context specific data processing. Different business scenarios might require different transformation approaches for the same data. Understanding how to implement conditional logic efficiently helps handle diverse business requirements while maintaining code clarity.

Feature engineering represents a critical aspect of advanced transformation. Creating meaningful derived features often requires combining multiple data elements, applying business knowledge, and considering temporal relationships. Understanding feature creation techniques helps extract maximum value from raw business data.

String manipulation beyond basic cleaning enables sophisticated text processing. Pattern matching, regular expressions, and text parsing extract structured information from unstructured text data. These capabilities prove particularly valuable when dealing with customer feedback, product descriptions, or transaction notes.

Mathematical transformations beyond basic arithmetic support complex business calculations. Logarithmic transformations, polynomial features, and trigonometric functions might be necessary for specific business metrics. Understanding when and how to apply mathematical transformations ensures meaningful results.

Binning and discretization techniques enable meaningful grouping of continuous data. Custom bin boundaries based on business logic, adaptive binning based on data distribution, and multiple binning approaches for different analyses provide flexibility in data representation.

Complex data type conversions handle special business data formats. Custom date formats, industry specific notations, and specialized business codes require careful handling. Developing robust conversion procedures ensures accurate interpretation of business specific data formats.

Outlier transformation requires balance between statistical validity and business reality. Different business contexts might require different approaches to outlier handling. Understanding various transformation techniques for outliers helps maintain data validity while preserving important business information.

Distribution transformations modify data characteristics for specific analytical requirements. Skewed business metrics might need transformation for statistical analysis. Understanding distribution modification techniques helps prepare data for various analytical methods.

Dimensionality reduction techniques help manage complex business datasets. Principal component analysis, feature selection, and other reduction methods might be necessary for efficient analysis. Understanding when and how to apply dimensionality reduction ensures effective data handling.

Interactive transformations enable exploratory analysis and refinement. Business analysts often need to experiment with different transformation approaches. Developing efficient workflows for interactive transformation supports iterative analysis and insight discovery.

Transformation pipelines combine multiple steps into coherent workflows. Complex business data often requires sequences of transformations. Understanding pipeline construction and management ensures reproducible and maintainable transformation processes.

Memory efficient transformations become crucial with large business datasets. Some transformations might require careful implementation to handle memory constraints. Understanding memory efficient approaches ensures practical implementation of complex transformations.

Performance optimization of transformations supports production implementation. Complex transformations might need optimization for regular execution. Understanding optimization techniques ensures practical application of advanced transformations.

Documentation of transformation logic preserves business knowledge and enables maintenance. Complex transformations often embed important business rules and assumptions. Maintaining clear documentation ensures long term usefulness of transformation implementations.

Testing transformation accuracy requires comprehensive verification. Complex transformations need testing across various scenarios and edge cases. Developing thorough testing procedures ensures reliable transformation results.

Version control for transformations maintains consistency and enables updates. As business requirements evolve, transformations might need modification. Proper version control ensures systematic management of transformation changes.

This comprehensive approach to advanced data transformation techniques provides business analysts with tools to handle complex data processing requirements while maintaining efficiency and reliability. Understanding and applying these techniques enables sophisticated business analytics while ensuring practical implementation in production environments.

16. Reshaping and Pivoting Data

Reshaping and pivoting data represents a fundamental skill in business analytics, enabling analysts to transform data structures to suit different analytical needs and reporting requirements. Understanding these techniques allows for efficient data manipulation and insightful analysis of business metrics.

Data reshaping fundamentally alters how information is organized without changing the underlying data. In business contexts, data often arrives in formats optimized for storage or transaction processing rather than analysis. The ability to restructure this data efficiently becomes crucial for extracting meaningful insights.

Wide to long format conversion represents a common reshaping operation in business analytics. Transaction data might arrive with multiple metrics spread across columns, requiring transformation into a more analysis friendly format. Understanding how to efficiently perform this conversion while maintaining data integrity enables proper time series analysis, customer behavior studies, and performance tracking.

Long to wide format transformation often supports reporting and comparative analysis. Customer feedback collected over time might need restructuring to show trends across different metrics simultaneously. Mastering these transformations enables creation of intuitive dashboards and comprehensive reports that business stakeholders can easily interpret.

Pivoting operations reorganize data to create summary views and cross tabulations. Sales data might need restructuring to show product performance across different regions or time periods. Understanding pivoting techniques enables quick creation of summary tables that highlight important business patterns and relationships.

Multi index handling becomes crucial when dealing with hierarchical business data. Organizations often track metrics across multiple dimensions such as product categories, geographic regions, and time periods. Managing multi level indexes efficiently enables complex analysis while maintaining data organization.

Dynamic reshaping operations adapt to changing data structures. Business data sources might evolve over time, adding new categories or metrics. Developing flexible reshaping approaches ensures analytical processes remain robust as data structures change.

Aggregation during reshaping enables efficient data summarization. Business metrics often need consolidation at different levels while restructuring data. Understanding how to combine reshaping with aggregation produces efficient analytical workflows.

Memory efficient reshaping techniques become important with large datasets. Some business datasets might be too large for simple reshaping operations. Understanding memory efficient approaches ensures practical implementation of necessary transformations.

Handling missing values during reshaping requires careful consideration. Business data often contains gaps that need appropriate handling during restructuring. Developing systematic approaches to missing value handling during reshaping ensures reliable results.

Preserving data types through reshaping operations maintains data integrity. Different business metrics might have specific data type requirements that need preservation during restructuring. Understanding type preservation techniques ensures accurate analysis after reshaping.

Combining multiple reshaping operations enables complex transformations. Business requirements might necessitate several restructuring steps to achieve desired formats. Understanding how to efficiently combine reshaping operations produces effective data preparation workflows.

Validation after reshaping ensures transformation accuracy. Complex restructuring operations need verification to ensure data integrity. Developing systematic validation approaches confirms successful reshaping operations.

Documentation of reshaping logic preserves knowledge and enables maintenance. Complex restructuring often involves important business rules and assumptions. Maintaining clear documentation ensures long term usefulness of reshaping implementations.

Performance optimization becomes crucial for regularly executed reshaping operations. Some business processes might require frequent data restructuring. Understanding optimization techniques ensures efficient execution of necessary transformations.

Error handling during reshaping operations ensures robust processes. Complex restructuring might encounter unexpected data conditions. Developing comprehensive error handling ensures reliable operation of reshaping processes.

Integration with other data transformation steps creates efficient workflows. Reshaping often forms part of larger data preparation processes. Understanding how to effectively combine reshaping with other transformations enables streamlined data preparation.

Testing reshaping operations across different scenarios ensures reliability. Business data might present various edge cases that need proper handling. Developing thorough testing procedures confirms robust reshaping implementations.

Version control for reshaping operations maintains consistency and enables updates. As business requirements evolve, restructuring approaches might need modification. Proper version control ensures systematic management of reshaping changes.

This comprehensive approach to data reshaping and pivoting provides business analysts with tools to efficiently transform data structures while maintaining data integrity and enabling meaningful analysis. Understanding and applying these techniques supports sophisticated business analytics while ensuring practical implementation in production environments.

17. Aggregation Methods for Business Metrics

Aggregation methods form a cornerstone of business metrics analysis, enabling organizations to derive meaningful insights from large volumes of raw data. Understanding and effectively implementing aggregation techniques allows analysts to transform detailed transactional data into actionable business intelligence.

Basic aggregation functions serve as the foundation for business metrics calculation. Sum operations help track total sales, revenue, and costs across different business dimensions. Mean calculations provide insights into average customer spending, typical transaction values, and standard performance metrics. Count operations reveal transaction volumes, customer interactions, and activity levels across business segments.

Advanced aggregation methods enable sophisticated business analysis. Weighted averages might account for varying importance of different business factors. Rolling calculations track moving averages of key performance indicators over time. Cumulative aggregations monitor progressive totals throughout business periods.

Grouping operations organize data for meaningful aggregation. Business metrics often require analysis across multiple dimensions such as product categories, customer segments, or geographic regions. Understanding effective grouping strategies ensures appropriate aggregation at relevant business levels.

Multiple level aggregation handles hierarchical business structures. Organizations typically analyze metrics at various organizational levels, from individual transactions to department, region, and company wide summaries. Mastering multi level aggregation techniques enables comprehensive business performance analysis.

Custom aggregation functions address specific business requirements. Standard aggregations might not capture unique business rules or specialized calculations. Developing custom aggregation methods ensures business specific metrics accurately reflect organizational needs.

Time based aggregation supports periodic business reporting. Daily, weekly, monthly, and yearly aggregations form the basis of regular business reviews. Understanding temporal aggregation techniques enables efficient creation of period based performance reports.

Conditional aggregation implements business logic in calculations. Different metrics might require varying calculation approaches based on business conditions. Implementing conditional aggregation ensures appropriate handling of diverse business scenarios.

Efficient aggregation techniques become crucial with large datasets. Business data volumes continue growing, requiring optimized approaches to aggregation. Understanding performance considerations ensures practical implementation of necessary calculations.

Missing value handling during aggregation maintains calculation accuracy. Business data often contains gaps that need appropriate treatment during aggregation. Developing systematic approaches to missing value handling ensures reliable metric calculations.

Parallel aggregation techniques leverage modern computing capabilities. Large scale business analytics might benefit from distributed processing. Understanding parallel aggregation approaches enables efficient processing of substantial data volumes.

Incremental aggregation supports real time business monitoring. Some business contexts require continuous metric updates. Implementing incremental aggregation enables efficient handling of streaming data scenarios.

Cross sectional aggregation enables comparative business analysis. Organizations often need to compare performance across different business dimensions simultaneously. Mastering cross sectional aggregation techniques supports comprehensive business assessment.

Statistical aggregation methods provide deeper analytical insights. Beyond basic summaries, businesses benefit from statistical measures of variation, distribution, and correlation. Understanding statistical aggregation enables sophisticated business analysis.

Aggregation result validation ensures calculation accuracy. Complex business metrics require verification to confirm correct implementation. Developing systematic validation approaches confirms reliable aggregation results.

Documentation of aggregation methods preserves organizational knowledge. Business metrics often incorporate important rules and assumptions. Maintaining clear documentation ensures long term usefulness of metric calculations.

Integration with visualization systems enables effective communication. Business metrics typically feed into reporting dashboards and presentations. Understanding how to structure aggregations for visualization ensures effective information delivery.

Error handling during aggregation ensures robust metric calculation. Complex business calculations might encounter unexpected conditions. Developing comprehensive error handling ensures reliable metric generation.

Version control for aggregation methods maintains consistency. As business requirements evolve, calculation approaches might need modification. Proper version control ensures systematic management of metric changes.

Performance monitoring of aggregation processes enables optimization. Regular metric calculation might consume significant resources. Understanding performance characteristics enables efficient implementation of business calculations.

Memory management becomes crucial for large scale aggregations. Some business metrics might involve substantial data volumes.

Understanding memory efficient approaches ensures practical implementation of necessary calculations.

The comprehensive understanding of aggregation methods provides business analysts with tools to effectively transform detailed data into meaningful business metrics. These techniques support sophisticated business analytics while ensuring practical implementation in production environments. Through careful consideration of business requirements, performance characteristics, and implementation details, organizations can develop robust and efficient aggregation processes that deliver valuable business insights.

18. Merging and Joining Datasets

Merging and joining datasets represents a critical skill in business analytics, where insights often emerge from combining information across multiple sources. Understanding various joining techniques and their appropriate application enables analysts to create comprehensive views of business operations and performance.

Traditional database style joins form the foundation of dataset combination. Inner joins connect records with matching keys across datasets, ensuring data consistency but potentially excluding unmatched records. Left and right joins preserve all records from one dataset while incorporating matching records from another, useful when maintaining complete records from a primary dataset. Full outer joins retain all records from both datasets, filling unmatched entries with missing values.

Key selection proves crucial for successful dataset merging. Business datasets often contain multiple potential joining fields, requiring careful consideration of appropriate connection points. Customer identification numbers, transaction dates, product codes, or combinations thereof might serve as joining keys depending on analytical requirements.

Data preparation before merging ensures successful combination. Key fields must maintain consistent formats across datasets. Standardizing date formats, text case sensitivity, and numerical precision prevents joining failures. Removing duplicate keys within individual datasets prevents unintended record multiplication during joining operations.

Multiple dataset merging requires strategic planning. Business analyses frequently involve more than two datasets. Understanding efficient approaches to combining multiple sources prevents performance issues and ensures accurate results. Sequential joining operations might require careful ordering to maintain data integrity.

Handling conflicting information across datasets demands systematic approaches. Different sources might contain contradictory information for the same business entity. Developing clear rules for conflict resolution ensures consistent results. Latest record precedence, source reliability hierarchy, or custom business rules might guide conflict resolution.

Performance optimization becomes crucial with large datasets. Joining operations can consume significant computational resources. Understanding memory efficient approaches, such as chunked processing or database style operations, ensures practical implementation. Index optimization supports efficient joining operations.

Missing value treatment during joining operations affects analysis results. Business datasets rarely provide perfect matching across sources. Understanding implications of various missing value handling approaches ensures appropriate analytical outcomes. Filling missing values, filtering incomplete records, or maintaining missing indicators might suit different analytical requirements.

Validation of joined datasets ensures result accuracy. Comparing record counts, checking key business metrics, and verifying sample records confirms successful combination. Systematic validation approaches prevent analytical errors from incorrect dataset joining.

Time based joining handles temporal business data. Many business analyses require combining information across time periods. Understanding appropriate approaches to temporal joining ensures accurate historical analysis. Rolling window operations, period matching, and time range overlaps present common temporal joining scenarios.

Conditional joining implements business logic during combination. Some analyses require joining datasets only when specific conditions are met. Understanding conditional joining approaches enables implementation of complex business rules during data combination.

Many to many relationship handling requires careful consideration. Business datasets often contain complex relationships between entities. Understanding appropriate approaches to many to many joining prevents data explosion while maintaining analytical accuracy.

Memory efficient joining techniques support large scale analysis. Some business scenarios involve combining substantial datasets. Understanding memory efficient approaches ensures practical implementation of necessary data combinations.

Cross database joining enables comprehensive business analysis. Organizations often maintain data in different database systems. Understanding approaches to combining data across database platforms supports enterprise wide analytics.

Real time data joining supports dynamic business monitoring. Some scenarios require combining streaming data with existing datasets. Understanding real time joining approaches enables timely business insights.

Documentation of joining operations preserves analytical knowledge. Complex data combinations often incorporate important business rules and assumptions. Maintaining clear documentation ensures reproducibility and knowledge transfer.

Error handling during joining operations ensures robust analysis. Complex data combinations might encounter unexpected conditions. Developing comprehensive error handling ensures reliable analytical results.

Version control for joining operations maintains consistency. As business requirements evolve, data combination approaches might need modification. Proper version control ensures systematic management of analytical changes.

Performance monitoring of joining operations enables optimization. Regular data combination might consume significant resources. Understanding performance characteristics enables efficient implementation of necessary analytics.

The mastery of dataset merging and joining techniques provides analysts with essential tools for comprehensive business analytics. Through careful consideration of business requirements, technical constraints, and implementation details, organizations can develop robust and efficient data combination processes that support sophisticated business insights.

19. Complex Dataset Integration

Complex dataset integration builds upon basic merging and joining operations to address more sophisticated business data challenges. Modern organizations frequently need to combine data from numerous disparate sources, each with its own structure, format, and business context. Successfully integrating these diverse datasets requires a systematic approach that goes beyond simple joining operations.

Data source evaluation forms the first critical step in complex integration. Each source must be assessed for data quality, completeness, update frequency, and business relevance. Understanding these characteristics helps determine appropriate integration strategies and prioritize data cleaning efforts. Sources might include internal databases, external vendor feeds, public datasets, or real time streams.

Schema reconciliation presents a significant challenge in complex integration. Different systems often use varying naming conventions, data types, and structural organization. Creating a unified schema requires careful mapping of fields across sources while preserving business meaning. Field name standardization, data type conversion, and structural transformation often prove necessary.

Business rule implementation ensures meaningful integration. Organizations typically maintain complex rules governing data relationships and transformations. These rules must be systematically implemented during integration. Validation checks, transformation logic, and relationship enforcement maintain data integrity throughout the integration process.

Hierarchical data integration requires specialized approaches. Business data often contains complex hierarchical relationships between entities. Parent child relationships, organizational structures, and product categorizations present common hierarchical integration challenges. Proper handling ensures meaningful analysis across organizational levels.

Historical data integration presents temporal challenges. Different systems might maintain varying historical coverage or update frequencies. Reconciling temporal differences while maintaining analytical accuracy requires careful consideration. Version tracking, effective dating, and temporal alignment strategies support accurate historical analysis.

Reference data management supports consistent integration. Organizations typically maintain master data for customers, products, locations, or other key entities. Proper reference data management ensures consistent entity identification across integrated datasets. Version control, update procedures, and conflict resolution mechanisms maintain reference data integrity.

Data quality monitoring becomes crucial in complex integration. Multiple data sources increase opportunities for quality issues. Implementing comprehensive quality monitoring ensures early detection of integration problems. Automated checks, exception reporting, and quality metrics support ongoing data reliability.

Performance optimization requires careful consideration in complex integration. Combining multiple large datasets can strain computational resources. Efficient processing strategies, such as parallel processing, incremental updates, or streaming integration, ensure practical implementation. Resource monitoring and optimization support sustainable integration processes.

Error handling becomes more sophisticated with complex integration. Multiple data sources increase potential failure points. Comprehensive error handling ensures graceful recovery from various failure scenarios. Error logging, notification systems, and recovery procedures maintain integration reliability.

Metadata management supports complex integration processes. Understanding data lineage, transformation rules, and quality characteristics becomes crucial with multiple sources. Proper metadata management ensures transparency and maintainability of integration processes. Documentation systems, version control, and change management support long term success.

Security considerations become paramount in complex integration. Different data sources might have varying security requirements or access restrictions. Implementing appropriate security measures ensures compliance while enabling necessary integration. Access control, encryption, and audit trails protect sensitive information.

Scalability planning supports growing integration needs. Business requirements often expand over time, requiring additional data sources or increased processing capacity. Designing scalable integration architecture ensures long term viability. Modular design, cloud infrastructure, and performance monitoring support future growth.

Change management processes support evolving integration requirements. Business needs and data sources frequently change over time. Systematic change management ensures controlled evolution of integration processes. Impact analysis, testing procedures, and deployment controls maintain integration reliability.

Documentation becomes critical for complex integration. Multiple stakeholders need to understand various aspects of integrated data. Comprehensive documentation supports effective use and maintenance of integrated datasets. Technical specifications, business rules, and user guides enable proper utilization.

Testing strategies ensure integration reliability. Complex integration requires comprehensive testing across multiple scenarios. Unit testing, integration testing, and end to end validation confirm proper functionality. Test automation supports ongoing quality assurance.

Monitoring systems track integration health. Regular operation of complex integration requires active monitoring. Performance metrics, error rates, and data quality indicators provide early warning of potential issues. Alerting systems enable prompt response to integration problems.

Recovery procedures ensure business continuity. Complex integration systems occasionally encounter failures. Well defined recovery procedures ensure minimal business impact. Backup systems, failover procedures, and disaster recovery plans maintain critical operations.

The successful implementation of complex dataset integration requires careful attention to numerous technical and business considerations. Through systematic approaches to these challenges, organizations can create reliable and maintainable integration processes that support sophisticated business analytics. Regular review and optimization of integration processes ensures continued effectiveness as business needs evolve.

20. Time Series Data Fundamentals

Time series data forms a crucial component of modern business analytics, presenting unique characteristics and challenges that require specialized handling approaches. Understanding these fundamentals enables analysts to effectively process and analyze temporal data patterns that drive business insights.

Time series data consists of observations collected sequentially over time, typically at regular intervals. Business examples include daily sales figures, hourly website traffic, monthly inventory levels, or quarterly financial metrics. The temporal ordering of these observations creates inherent dependencies that distinguish time series from other data types.

The fundamental structure of time series data requires careful consideration during processing. Each observation must maintain its precise temporal context, including date, time, and frequency information. Python's datetime and pandas timestamp objects provide robust handling of these temporal elements, supporting various time zones, frequencies, and calendar calculations.

Proper time series data organization begins with establishing consistent datetime indexing. Converting temporal information into standardized datetime format ensures reliable processing. Pandas DatetimeIndex functionality supports various input formats while maintaining temporal relationships. This foundation enables sophisticated time based operations and analysis.

Frequency management plays a vital role in time series processing. Business data often arrives at different frequencies, from millisecond trading data to annual reports. Understanding and standardizing these frequencies supports meaningful analysis. Pandas provides comprehensive frequency handling through various offset aliases, enabling consistent temporal processing.

Missing data handling requires special attention in time series contexts. Temporal gaps might represent actual missing observations or expected absence of activity. Forward filling, backward filling, or interpolation methods must consider the temporal nature of the data. Business context often determines appropriate handling strategies.

Time series resampling supports analysis at different temporal granularities. Upsampling to higher frequencies or downsampling to lower frequencies requires careful consideration of aggregation methods. Sum, mean, first, last, or custom aggregations maintain business meaning while changing temporal resolution.

Rolling windows calculations enable analysis of moving patterns in time series data. Computing moving averages, rolling sums, or custom metrics provides insight into temporal trends. Window size selection balances sensitivity to recent changes with stability of metrics. Business requirements often guide these analytical choices.

Shifting operations support lead/lag analysis in time series data. Comparing current observations with past or future values enables trend analysis and forecasting preparation. Proper handling of temporal boundaries ensures reliable shifted calculations. These operations often support business planning and prediction activities.

Seasonal patterns frequently appear in business time series data. Daily, weekly, monthly, or annual cycles affect many business metrics. Identifying and accounting for these patterns supports meaningful analysis. Seasonal decomposition techniques separate underlying trends from cyclical variations.

Time zone handling becomes crucial in global business operations. Data collected across different time zones requires careful synchronization. Pandas provides robust time zone support through conversion and localization functions. Proper time zone management ensures accurate temporal analysis across geographical regions.

Period calculations support business specific time measurements. Fiscal years, business quarters, or custom periods often differ from calendar divisions. Pandas period functionality enables consistent handling of these business temporal units. Custom period definitions support organization specific reporting requirements.

Time based joining operations combine multiple time series while maintaining temporal relationships. Proper temporal alignment ensures meaningful combination of different metrics. Merge asof operations handle non exactly matching timestamps. These capabilities support comprehensive business analysis across multiple time series.

Performance considerations become important with large time series datasets. Efficient datetime handling, appropriate indexing, and optimized calculations ensure practical processing. Pandas provides various optimization options for time series operations. Memory management strategies support processing of extensive temporal data.

Data quality validation for time series requires temporal context. Checking for unexpected gaps, duplicate timestamps, or anomalous patterns supports reliable analysis. Automated validation procedures incorporate temporal relationships. Regular quality monitoring ensures ongoing reliability of time series data.

Documentation of time series processing becomes essential for maintaining analytical consistency. Recording frequency assumptions, handling of special cases, and processing decisions supports reproducible analysis. Clear documentation enables proper interpretation and future maintenance of time series analytics.

Time series visualization preparation requires careful consideration of temporal aspects. Proper datetime formatting, axis scaling, and temporal aggregation support effective visual analysis. Various plotting libraries provide specialized time series visualization capabilities. These visual tools support communication of temporal patterns and trends.

The fundamentals of time series data handling provide essential capabilities for business analytics. Understanding these concepts enables effective processing of temporal business data, supporting sophisticated analysis and decision making. Regular review of time series handling practices ensures continued effectiveness as business requirements evolve.

Business applications of time series fundamentals span numerous domains. Financial analysis relies heavily on temporal patterns in market data. Sales forecasting depends on historical time series analysis. Operations monitoring requires real time processing of temporal metrics. These applications demonstrate the broad relevance of time series capabilities in modern business analytics.

21. Time Series Analysis for Business

Time series analysis forms a cornerstone of modern business analytics, providing crucial insights into patterns, trends, and seasonal variations that drive business performance. This analysis extends beyond basic temporal data handling to sophisticated techniques that reveal underlying business dynamics and support strategic decision making.

Trend analysis serves as a fundamental component of time series business analytics. By examining long term directional movements in business metrics, analysts can identify sustained patterns of growth, decline, or stability. These trends often reveal underlying business dynamics such as market expansion, competitive pressures, or structural changes in customer behavior. Detrending techniques help separate these long term movements from shorter term fluctuations, enabling clearer analysis of other temporal patterns.

Seasonal decomposition provides essential insights into recurring patterns in business data. Many business metrics exhibit regular cyclical variations daily, weekly, monthly, or annually. Understanding these patterns supports operational planning, resource allocation, and forecasting. Advanced decomposition methods separate time series into trend, seasonal, and residual components, enabling focused analysis of each aspect. This decomposition supports more accurate forecasting and anomaly detection.

Autocorrelation analysis reveals temporal dependencies in business metrics. Understanding how past values influence future observations helps in forecasting and pattern recognition. Different business metrics exhibit varying degrees of temporal dependency, from highly correlated financial indicators to more independent operational metrics. These relationships inform modeling choices and prediction strategies.

Moving average analysis smooths short term fluctuations to reveal underlying patterns. Different types of moving averages, from simple to exponentially weighted, serve various analytical purposes. Shorter windows maintain sensitivity to recent changes while longer windows reveal long term patterns. Selection of appropriate moving average parameters depends on specific business requirements and the nature of the analyzed metrics.

Cross correlation analysis examines relationships between different time series metrics. Understanding how changes in one business metric relate to future changes in another supports casual analysis and prediction. Lead lag relationships between sales, marketing efforts, and customer behavior inform strategic planning. These temporal relationships often reveal complex business dynamics not apparent in static analysis.

Volatility analysis measures the stability and variability of business metrics over time. Different business domains exhibit varying levels of natural volatility. Understanding these patterns supports risk assessment and planning. Techniques like rolling standard deviation and exponentially weighted variance provide insights into changing volatility patterns.

Change point detection identifies significant shifts in business metrics. These might represent structural changes in the business environment, competitive actions, or internal policy changes. Various algorithmic approaches help identify both sudden and gradual changes. Understanding these transition points supports adaptive business strategies and retrospective analysis.

Anomaly detection within time series context considers both magnitude and temporal pattern deviations. Business metrics often exhibit complex normal variations that must be considered when identifying true anomalies. Combined analysis of level, trend, and seasonal patterns supports more accurate anomaly detection. These capabilities enable proactive identification of business issues or opportunities.

Forecasting preparation requires careful consideration of historical patterns and business context. Different forecasting methods suit different types of time series patterns. Understanding the stability of trends, consistency of seasonal patterns, and presence of special events supports appropriate model selection. Proper separation of training and validation periods ensures reliable forecast evaluation.

Temporal aggregation strategies support analysis at different business relevant time scales. Aggregating from detailed to summary levels requires careful consideration of business meaning. Different metrics might require different aggregation methods, from simple sums to weighted averages or complex calculations. These aggregation choices significantly impact subsequent analysis and interpretation.

Business cycle analysis examines longer term patterns beyond seasonal variations. Economic cycles, technology adoption curves, and industry specific patterns influence many business metrics. Understanding these longer term patterns supports strategic planning and risk management. Combined analysis of multiple metrics often reveals complex cycle interactions.

Intervention analysis examines the impact of specific events or actions on time series patterns. Marketing campaigns, policy changes, or external events can significantly impact business metrics. Proper analysis separates these intervention effects from underlying patterns. These insights support evaluation of business actions and planning of future interventions.

Quality control applications of time series analysis monitor business processes over time. Control charts and other monitoring techniques consider both level and pattern changes. Understanding normal process variation supports identification of significant deviations. These applications enable proactive management of business operations.

Performance measurement often requires time series context for proper interpretation. Year over year comparisons, trailing twelve month calculations, and other temporal metrics provide business relevant measures. Proper handling of special events, seasonal patterns, and trend changes ensures meaningful performance evaluation. These measurements support objective assessment of business performance.

The application of time series analysis techniques to business problems requires careful consideration of context and requirements. Different business domains and metrics require different analytical approaches. Understanding these applications enables effective selection and implementation of appropriate techniques. Regular review of analytical approaches ensures continued alignment with business needs.

22. Seasonal Decomposition and Trending

Seasonal decomposition and trending analysis provide essential frameworks for understanding the cyclical and directional patterns within business data. These techniques allow analysts to separate complex time series data into distinct components that reveal underlying business dynamics and support more accurate forecasting and decision making.

The fundamental concept of seasonal decomposition involves breaking a time series into its core components: trend, seasonal patterns, residuals, and sometimes cyclical elements. This decomposition enables analysts to examine each component independently, leading to clearer insights into the driving forces behind business metrics. The trend component represents the long term movement in the data, while seasonal patterns capture regular, predictable fluctuations that occur at fixed intervals.

Several mathematical approaches support seasonal decomposition, with multiplicative and additive models being the most common. Multiplicative decomposition assumes that seasonal variations increase proportionally with the trend level, making it particularly suitable for business metrics that show larger seasonal swings during peak periods. Additive decomposition, conversely, assumes consistent seasonal variations regardless of the trend level, often applying better to metrics with stable seasonal patterns.

The implementation of seasonal decomposition begins with careful consideration of the time series characteristics. Analysts must determine the appropriate seasonal period, which might be daily, weekly, monthly, or yearly, depending on the business context. For retail sales, weekly and yearly seasonal patterns often dominate, while manufacturing metrics might show stronger daily or monthly patterns. The selection of decomposition method and seasonal period significantly impacts the quality of insights generated.

Trending analysis extends beyond simple linear patterns to encompass various types of growth and decline patterns. Exponential trends often characterize rapid growth phases in business metrics, while logarithmic trends might better represent maturing markets or products. Polynomial trends capture more complex patterns with multiple inflection points, useful for modeling business cycles or product lifecycles. The identification and characterization of these trend patterns support strategic planning and forecasting.

Advanced trending techniques incorporate change point detection to identify significant shifts in the underlying pattern. These change points might represent structural changes in the business environment, competitive actions, or internal policy changes. Methods like piecewise regression and Bayesian change point detection help identify both sudden and gradual transitions in trend patterns. Understanding these transition points supports adaptive business strategies and helps explain historical performance patterns.

Detrending techniques play a crucial role in isolating seasonal and cyclical patterns from the underlying trend. Various methods, from simple linear detrending to more sophisticated techniques like Hodrick Prescott filtering, help separate long term movements from shorter term variations. The choice of detrending method depends on the nature of the trend and the specific requirements of subsequent analysis.

The analysis of detrended data reveals seasonal patterns more clearly, enabling better understanding of regular business cycles. These patterns might reflect consumer behavior, weather effects, or institutional factors like fiscal years or reporting periods. Quantifying the strength and stability of seasonal patterns supports operational planning and resource allocation. Changes in seasonal patterns over time might indicate evolving market dynamics or shifting business conditions.

Residual analysis after decomposition provides insights into the stability and predictability of business metrics. Strong seasonal patterns and clear trends result in smaller, more random residuals, while weak patterns lead to larger, more structured residuals. The characteristics of these residuals inform confidence levels for forecasts and help identify periods of unusual volatility or uncertainty.

The combination of trending and seasonal analysis supports more sophisticated business applications. Marketing teams can better plan campaigns by understanding both long term market trends and seasonal buying patterns. Operations managers can optimize resource allocation by considering both growth trends and seasonal capacity requirements. Financial analysts can improve forecasting accuracy by separately modeling trend and seasonal components.

Calendar adjustments often form an important part of seasonal analysis in business contexts. Variations in trading days, holiday effects, and special events can significantly impact business metrics. Proper adjustment for these calendar effects improves the quality of seasonal decomposition and trending analysis. These adjustments become particularly important when comparing performance across different time periods or between regions with different calendar patterns.

The integration of external factors into trending and seasonal analysis provides additional context for business interpretation. Economic indicators, weather data, or competitive actions might explain variations in both trend and seasonal patterns. Understanding these relationships supports more nuanced analysis and better informed decision making. The incorporation of external factors often improves the accuracy of forecasting models based on trend and seasonal patterns.

Modern computational techniques have expanded the capabilities of trending and seasonal analysis. Machine learning approaches can identify complex patterns and relationships that might not be apparent in traditional decomposition methods. These advanced techniques often provide more accurate results when dealing with noisy data or complex seasonal patterns. However, the interpretability of traditional decomposition methods remains valuable for business understanding and communication.

The effective application of trending and seasonal analysis requires careful consideration of business context and requirements. Different industries and metrics require different analytical approaches. Regular review and adjustment of analysis methods ensures continued alignment with business needs. The combination of traditional decomposition methods with modern analytical techniques provides a robust framework for understanding and predicting business patterns.

23. Customer Data Processing

Customer data processing forms a critical foundation for modern business analytics, enabling organizations to transform raw customer information into actionable insights that drive strategic decision making. The ability to effectively process, clean, and structure customer data determines the success of downstream analytics initiatives and customer relationship management efforts.

The journey of customer data processing begins with understanding the diverse sources and formats of customer information. Organizations typically collect customer data through multiple channels including point of sale systems, website interactions, mobile applications, customer service records, and third party data providers. Each source presents unique processing challenges, from inconsistent formatting to varying data quality standards. The first step in effective processing involves standardizing these diverse inputs into a coherent, unified structure.

Data quality assessment represents a crucial early stage in customer data processing. Common quality issues in customer datasets include duplicate records, inconsistent naming conventions, outdated information, and incomplete profiles. Implementing robust deduplication processes helps identify and merge duplicate customer records while preserving the most current and accurate information. This often involves sophisticated matching algorithms that can recognize variations in name spellings, address formats, and other identifying information.

Contact information processing requires particular attention due to its critical role in customer communications. Address standardization ensures consistent formatting and validates addresses against postal databases. Email address validation confirms format correctness and checks for common typing errors. Phone number processing includes format standardization, country code validation, and verification of number validity. These standardization processes improve data quality while reducing communication failures and associated costs.

Customer demographic data often requires extensive cleaning and normalization. Age data might need to be derived from birth dates or grouped into meaningful segments. Gender information frequently contains various representations that need standardization. Income data might require currency conversion and normalization across different regions. Occupation and industry classifications often need mapping to standardized taxonomies to enable meaningful analysis.

Transaction history processing forms another crucial component of customer data management. This involves cleaning and structuring purchase records, return information, and payment data. Transaction timestamps need standardization across time zones and consistent formatting. Product codes and categories require normalization to enable accurate analysis of purchasing patterns. Payment method information needs cleaning and categorization to support financial analysis and fraud detection.

Customer interaction data from multiple channels requires integration and standardization. This includes processing customer service records, social media interactions, website behavior data, and mobile app usage information. The challenge lies in creating a unified view of customer interactions while maintaining the context and specificity of each channel. Timestamp alignment, interaction categorization, and sentiment analysis often form part of this processing workflow.

Privacy considerations play a crucial role in customer data processing. Personal identifiable information (PII) requires special handling and appropriate masking or encryption. Geographic location data needs processing in compliance with regional privacy regulations. Consent management information must be tracked and integrated into processing workflows to ensure compliance with data protection requirements.

Historical data processing presents unique challenges in customer analytics. Old records might use different formats or contain obsolete information. Processing historical data requires careful handling of changed business rules, modified product categories, and evolved customer identifiers. Maintaining historical accuracy while enabling contemporary analysis requires sophisticated processing logic and careful documentation.

Customer segmentation preparation represents a critical processing step. This involves deriving and calculating variables that will serve as inputs to segmentation models. Behavioral metrics need standardization across different time periods. Value metrics require normalization across product lines and regions. Engagement metrics must be calculated consistently across different interaction channels.

Lifecycle status processing helps track customer relationships over time. This includes calculating customer tenure, identifying active versus inactive customers, and processing churn indicators. The definition and calculation of these status indicators require careful processing logic that accounts for business rules and industry specific considerations.

Reference data integration forms an important aspect of customer data processing. This includes mapping customer information to product catalogs, service offerings, and organizational hierarchies. Processing logic must handle changes in reference data over time while maintaining historical accuracy and enabling current analysis.

Data enrichment processing extends basic customer information with additional valuable attributes. This might involve processing third party demographic data, deriving lifestyle indicators from transaction patterns, or calculating propensity scores. The integration of enrichment data requires careful validation and quality control to maintain data integrity.

Performance optimization represents a crucial consideration in customer data processing. Large customer datasets require efficient processing algorithms and appropriate use of computational resources. Batch processing strategies need careful design to handle data volume while maintaining processing accuracy. Incremental processing approaches help manage regular data updates efficiently.

The automation of customer data processing workflows ensures consistency and reduces manual effort. This involves developing robust processing rules, implementing appropriate error handling, and establishing monitoring mechanisms. Documentation of processing logic and business rules supports maintenance and evolution of processing workflows over time.

Quality control mechanisms form an essential component of customer data processing. This includes implementing validation rules, monitoring data quality metrics, and establishing exception handling processes. Regular audits of processed data help identify issues and maintain processing effectiveness over time.

The success of customer data processing ultimately depends on its ability to support business objectives while maintaining data quality and compliance requirements. Regular review and refinement of processing workflows ensures continued alignment with evolving business needs and technological capabilities. The investment in robust customer data processing capabilities pays dividends through improved analytics accuracy and better business decision making.

24. Customer Segmentation Techniques

Customer segmentation techniques represent a critical advancement in data wrangling that transforms processed customer data into actionable business insights. The ability to effectively group customers based on meaningful characteristics enables targeted marketing, personalized service delivery, and strategic business planning. Understanding and implementing these techniques requires both technical proficiency and business acumen.

The foundation of customer segmentation begins with feature selection and preparation. This involves identifying and processing the key variables that will drive meaningful segmentation. Behavioral features might include purchase frequency, average transaction value, and product category preferences. Demographic features often encompass age, income level, and geographic location. Engagement metrics could include website visits, email response rates, and customer service interactions. The selection of these features must align with business objectives while ensuring data quality and completeness.

Recency, Frequency, and Monetary (RFM) analysis represents one of the most fundamental segmentation techniques in business analytics. This approach requires careful data preparation to calculate these three key metrics for each customer. Recency calculations must account for different time zones and business calendars. Frequency calculations need normalization across different purchase channels. Monetary calculations require currency standardization and handling of returns or refunds. The resulting RFM scores provide a foundation for customer value segmentation.

Behavioral segmentation techniques focus on patterns in customer actions and interactions. This requires processing historical transaction data to identify purchasing patterns, channel preferences, and response behaviors. Time-based patterns need careful handling to account for seasonality and trend effects. Product affinity analysis requires processing of basket data to identify common purchase combinations. Channel interaction data needs integration and standardization to create meaningful behavioral profiles.

Value-based segmentation techniques require sophisticated processing of financial data. This might involve calculating customer lifetime value, profitability metrics, or potential value scores. These calculations must account for various revenue streams, cost allocations, and time value of money considerations. Historical transaction data needs cleaning and standardization to ensure accurate value calculations. Future value prediction often requires processing of predictive indicators and risk factors.

Demographic segmentation remains important in many business contexts but requires careful data preparation. Age group definitions need standardization across different markets. Income bands require adjustment for regional economic differences. Occupation and industry classifications need mapping to consistent taxonomies. Geographic segmentation might involve processing of postal codes, census data, or custom territory definitions.

Machine learning based segmentation techniques introduce additional data preparation requirements. K-means clustering, one of the most common approaches, requires careful scaling and normalization of input variables. Hierarchical clustering needs distance metric calculations based on processed customer attributes. DBSCAN clustering requires density calculations based on standardized features. The success of these techniques depends heavily on the quality of feature preparation and preprocessing.

Lifecycle segmentation focuses on customer relationship stages and requires processing of temporal data. This involves calculating relationship duration, identifying key milestone events, and tracking status changes over time. Activity patterns need processing to identify active versus dormant customers. Churn risk indicators require calculation based on multiple behavioral signals. The processing logic must handle different relationship models across product lines or business units.

Need-based segmentation techniques require processing of both explicit and implicit indicators of customer requirements. Survey data needs cleaning and standardization. Product usage patterns require processing to infer customer needs. Service interaction records need analysis to identify common pain points. The integration of these various data sources requires careful handling of different data formats and quality levels.

Psychographic segmentation, while more complex, can be approached through careful processing of behavioral indicators and external data. Social media interaction data requires sentiment analysis and topic categorization. Lifestyle indicators need derivation from transaction patterns. External demographic data often requires integration and validation against internal customer records.

Dynamic segmentation approaches require regular reprocessing of customer data to maintain current segment assignments. This involves establishing efficient processing workflows that can handle incremental data updates. Change detection algorithms need implementation to identify significant shifts in customer behavior. Processing logic must maintain historical segment assignments while enabling current analysis.

The validation of segmentation results requires specific data processing techniques. This includes calculating segment stability metrics over time, processing internal homogeneity measures, and evaluating segment distinctiveness. Profile data for each segment needs summarization and statistical testing. The processing of validation metrics must account for different variable types and distributions.

Segmentation visualization preparation involves processing segment characteristics into presentable formats. This includes calculating segment sizes and compositions, preparing profile summaries, and processing comparative metrics. Time series data needs aggregation to show segment evolution. Geographic distribution data requires processing for mapping visualization.

The operationalization of customer segments requires processing to integrate segment assignments into operational systems. This involves creating efficient lookup mechanisms, processing segment change notifications, and maintaining segment history. The processing logic must handle real time segment assignment for new customers while maintaining batch processing capabilities for existing customers.

Multi-dimensional segmentation approaches require sophisticated processing to handle interactions between different segmentation schemes. This might involve processing cross-tabulations between value and behavioral segments, or analyzing migration patterns between lifecycle stages. The processing logic must maintain consistency across different segmentation dimensions while enabling flexible analysis.

Privacy considerations in segmentation require specific processing approaches. This includes anonymization of sensitive data before segmentation analysis, aggregation of results to prevent individual identification, and processing of consent requirements for different data uses. The processing logic must balance analytical utility with privacy protection requirements.

The success of customer segmentation techniques ultimately depends on the quality and sophistication of the underlying data processing. Regular refinement of processing workflows ensures segmentation results remain relevant and actionable. The investment in robust segmentation capabilities enables more effective customer relationship management and business strategy development.

25. Sales Data Transformation

Sales data transformation represents a critical aspect of business analytics, requiring sophisticated data processing techniques to convert raw sales data into actionable insights. This transformation process encompasses multiple stages, from initial data cleaning to advanced aggregation and standardization, ultimately enabling meaningful analysis of sales performance and trends.

The initial stage of sales data transformation typically involves standardizing transaction records across different sales channels and systems. Point of sale data, e-commerce transactions, and direct sales records often come in varying formats with inconsistent field names and data structures. Creating a unified sales dataset requires careful mapping of fields, standardization of product codes, and normalization of transaction identifiers. This process must account for different time zones, currency denominations, and regional variations in product naming conventions.

Transaction level data cleaning forms a crucial component of the transformation process. This includes handling duplicate transactions, validating sale amounts against product prices, and identifying anomalous transactions that might indicate data quality issues. Returns and refunds require special processing to ensure they are properly matched with original sales transactions. Cancelled orders need appropriate flagging and exclusion from certain analyses while maintaining their record for customer behavior insights.

Product hierarchy management represents another critical aspect of sales data transformation. Raw sales data often contains product information at the SKU level, but analysis frequently requires aggregation at different category levels. This necessitates the creation and maintenance of product hierarchy mappings, ensuring that each transaction can be analyzed at multiple levels of granularity. The transformation process must handle changes in product categorization over time while maintaining historical consistency.

Price and discount calculations require careful transformation logic. List prices, actual selling prices, and various types of discounts need standardization across different sales channels. Special pricing arrangements, bulk discounts, and promotional offers require proper attribution in the transformed data. The calculation of margin metrics needs to account for varying cost structures and allocation methods. Historical price changes must be tracked to enable accurate trend analysis.

Customer attribution in sales data presents unique transformation challenges. Transaction data needs to be linked with customer records, requiring matching logic that can handle variations in customer identification across channels. Business to business sales might need attribution to both company and contact level. The transformation process must maintain customer hierarchies while enabling analysis at different organizational levels.

Sales territory and channel attribution require specific transformation approaches. Geographic coding needs standardization across different regional definitions. Sales channel attribution must account for mixed channel transactions and proper credit allocation. Territory assignments need to handle changes over time while maintaining historical reporting consistency. The transformation process must support different territory hierarchies for various analytical purposes.

Time based transformations form a crucial component of sales data processing. This includes creating date hierarchies for different reporting periods, handling fiscal year definitions, and maintaining period to period comparisons. Seasonal adjustments might be required for certain analyses. The transformation process must account for business calendar definitions and holiday schedules across different regions.

Commission and compensation related transformations require careful handling of attribution rules. Sales credit allocation needs to account for team selling scenarios and split commissions. The transformation process must handle different compensation plan structures and maintain historical records for audit purposes. Special handling might be required for complex deals with multiple components or extended delivery schedules.

Quota and target related transformations support performance analysis. This involves processing of quota assignments at various organizational levels and time periods. The transformation logic must handle quota adjustments and maintain historical quota versions. Territory changes require special processing to maintain consistent performance metrics over time.

Integration with other business data requires specific transformation approaches. Sales data might need linking with inventory systems, financial records, or customer service data. The transformation process must handle different update frequencies and maintain referential integrity across systems. Integration points need validation to ensure consistent business rules application.

Performance metric calculations represent a key output of sales data transformation. This includes standard metrics like revenue, units sold, and margin, as well as derived metrics like year over year growth, market share, and sales velocity. The transformation process must handle different calculation methodologies while maintaining consistency across reporting periods.

Forecasting and planning support requires specific transformation techniques. Historical sales patterns need processing to support trend analysis and forecasting models. The transformation process must handle different forecasting methodologies and maintain versions of forward looking data. Actual versus forecast comparisons need consistent calculation methods.

Data quality monitoring requires ongoing transformation processes. This includes tracking of key quality metrics, identification of data anomalies, and validation of transformation rules. The process must generate alerts for potential data issues and maintain audit trails of data changes. Regular quality reporting ensures the reliability of transformed sales data.

Compliance and audit requirements necessitate specific transformation approaches. This includes maintaining transaction level detail while supporting aggregated reporting, tracking data lineage, and documenting transformation rules. The process must support regulatory reporting requirements and enable audit verification of sales results.

The success of sales data transformation ultimately depends on establishing robust, maintainable processes that can adapt to changing business requirements while ensuring data quality and consistency. Regular review and refinement of transformation logic ensures the resulting data continues to support effective business decision making.

26. Sales Performance Analytics

Sales performance analytics represents one of the most critical applications of data wrangling in business intelligence, providing organizations with deep insights into their revenue generation and sales effectiveness. This chapter explores the comprehensive approaches to analyzing sales performance data, from basic metrics calculation to advanced analytical techniques that drive strategic decision making.

The foundation of sales performance analytics lies in establishing clear and consistent measurement frameworks. Organizations must first define their key performance indicators (KPIs) that align with business objectives. These typically include revenue metrics, conversion rates, sales cycle duration, pipeline velocity, and win rates. The analysis framework must account for different sales channels, product lines, and customer segments while maintaining consistency in measurement approaches.

Revenue analysis forms the cornerstone of sales performance analytics. This involves examining revenue patterns across multiple dimensions including time periods, product categories, sales territories, and customer segments. Advanced analysis techniques incorporate factors such as seasonal adjustments, market conditions, and competitive dynamics to provide context to revenue performance. The examination of revenue mix and concentration helps identify dependencies and opportunities for diversification.

Sales pipeline analysis provides crucial insights into future performance potential. This involves analyzing conversion rates at each stage of the sales process, identifying bottlenecks, and predicting future revenue based on pipeline characteristics. Advanced analytics techniques can determine optimal pipeline coverage ratios, predict deal closure probabilities, and identify factors that influence deal progression through the pipeline stages.

Deal size and pricing analytics reveal important patterns in sales effectiveness. Analysis of average deal sizes across different segments, win rates by deal size, and pricing consistency provides insights into sales strategy effectiveness. Price elasticity analysis helps optimize pricing strategies, while discount analysis reveals the impact of pricing decisions on profitability. Advanced techniques can identify optimal price points and predict customer price sensitivity.

Sales productivity analytics focuses on measuring and optimizing sales force effectiveness. This includes analyzing metrics such as sales per representative, territory coverage efficiency, and activity levels. Advanced analysis techniques can identify best practices from top performers, optimize territory assignments, and predict the impact of different resource allocation strategies. Time-based analysis reveals patterns in sales productivity and helps identify opportunities for improvement.

Customer acquisition cost analysis provides crucial insights into sales efficiency. This involves calculating and analyzing the total cost of acquiring new customers, including marketing expenses, sales costs, and overhead allocations. Advanced analytics can determine optimal customer acquisition strategies, predict lifetime value potential, and identify the most cost-effective sales channels. Trend analysis reveals changes in acquisition efficiency over time.

Win/loss analysis represents a critical component of sales performance analytics. This involves examining factors that influence deal outcomes, including competitive dynamics, product features, pricing, and sales approach. Advanced techniques can identify patterns in successful deals, predict win probabilities, and recommend optimal sales strategies. The analysis of loss reasons provides valuable insights for product development and sales training.

Sales cycle analysis examines the time dimension of sales performance. This includes analyzing the duration of sales cycles across different segments, identifying factors that influence cycle length, and optimizing process efficiency. Advanced analytics can predict cycle durations, identify opportunities for acceleration, and optimize resource allocation based on cycle characteristics.

Territory performance analytics provides geographical insights into sales effectiveness. This involves analyzing performance variations across territories, identifying market potential, and optimizing territory assignments. Advanced techniques can predict territory potential, recommend territory adjustments, and optimize coverage patterns. The analysis of territory characteristics helps identify best practices and improvement opportunities.

Channel performance analytics examines the effectiveness of different sales channels. This involves analyzing metrics across direct sales, partner channels, e-commerce, and other go-to-market approaches. Advanced analytics can optimize channel mix, predict channel performance, and identify cross-channel synergies. The analysis of channel economics helps optimize resource allocation across channels.

Product mix analytics reveals patterns in product sales performance. This includes analyzing product line revenue contributions, cross-sell patterns, and product lifecycle performance. Advanced techniques can identify optimal product bundles, predict product demand patterns, and optimize inventory allocation. The analysis of product profitability helps guide product strategy decisions.

Sales team performance analytics focuses on human capital effectiveness. This involves analyzing individual and team performance metrics, identifying training needs, and optimizing compensation structures. Advanced analytics can predict sales representative success, recommend development interventions, and optimize team compositions. The analysis of performance patterns helps identify best practices for sales management.

The implementation of effective sales performance analytics requires robust data infrastructure, clear business rules, and sophisticated analytical capabilities. Organizations must ensure data quality, maintain consistent measurement approaches, and regularly validate analytical outputs. The integration of multiple data sources enhances analytical depth, while automated reporting systems ensure timely insight delivery.

Success in sales performance analytics ultimately depends on the organization's ability to turn analytical insights into actionable strategies. This requires clear communication of insights, effective change management processes, and regular feedback loops to refine analytical approaches. The continuous evolution of analytical capabilities ensures ongoing value creation from sales performance data.

27. Financial Data Cleaning

Financial data cleaning represents a critical foundation for accurate financial analysis and reporting in modern business environments. The integrity and reliability of financial data directly impact decision making at all levels of an organization, making proper data cleaning techniques essential for financial professionals and analysts.

The complexity of financial data presents unique challenges in the data cleaning process. Financial datasets often contain multiple currencies, varying accounting standards, complex transaction records, and intricate relationships between different financial statements. This complexity requires a systematic approach to data cleaning that preserves data accuracy while ensuring analytical usefulness.

Transaction data cleaning forms the first line of defense in financial data integrity. This process involves identifying and correcting transaction recording errors, duplicate entries, and misclassifications. Advanced pattern recognition techniques help identify unusual transactions that may indicate recording errors or require additional verification. The cleaning process must maintain the fundamental accounting principle of balanced books while correcting discrepancies.

Currency standardization represents a crucial aspect of financial data cleaning, particularly for organizations operating internationally. This involves converting transactions from multiple currencies into a standard reporting currency, accounting for exchange rate fluctuations, and maintaining proper historical rate applications for different types of transactions. The cleaning process must handle complex scenarios such as hedging transactions and currency revaluation impacts.

Account reconciliation data requires particular attention in the cleaning process. This involves matching transactions across different systems, identifying unreconciled items, and ensuring proper classification of reconciling differences. The cleaning process must maintain clear audit trails while standardizing reconciliation data formats for automated processing.

Financial statement element cleaning focuses on ensuring consistency and accuracy in balance sheet, income statement, and cash flow statement components. This involves standardizing account classifications, validating inter statement relationships, and ensuring proper roll forward of balance sheet accounts. The cleaning process must maintain the integrity of financial statement relationships while correcting data anomalies.

Chart of accounts data cleaning ensures proper account hierarchy maintenance and classification consistency. This involves standardizing account naming conventions, validating account relationships, and maintaining proper account mappings for reporting purposes. The cleaning process must handle organizational changes while maintaining historical consistency in account structures.

Cost allocation data presents unique cleaning challenges due to its complexity and business rule dependencies. This involves validating allocation keys, ensuring completeness of allocation bases, and maintaining proper allocation hierarchies. The cleaning process must handle changes in allocation methodologies while maintaining historical comparability.

Budget and forecast data cleaning ensures proper comparison with actual results. This involves standardizing forecast assumptions, validating projection methodologies, and ensuring consistent treatment of exceptional items. The cleaning process must maintain clear distinctions between actual and projected data while enabling meaningful variance analysis.

Tax related data requires specialized cleaning approaches to ensure compliance and accuracy. This involves validating tax classifications, ensuring proper jurisdiction assignments, and maintaining accurate tax basis calculations. The cleaning process must handle complex tax rules while maintaining proper documentation for audit purposes.

Investment portfolio data cleaning addresses the unique characteristics of investment instruments and performance measurements. This involves standardizing security identifiers, ensuring proper pricing data, and validating performance calculations. The cleaning process must handle complex investment structures while maintaining accurate risk and return measurements.

Intercompany transaction data requires careful cleaning to ensure proper elimination and consolidation. This involves identifying and matching intercompany transactions, validating elimination entries, and ensuring proper treatment of intercompany profit elimination. The cleaning process must maintain proper documentation of elimination logic while ensuring accurate consolidated results.

Audit trail data cleaning ensures proper documentation and traceability of financial transactions. This involves standardizing audit log formats, maintaining proper change documentation, and ensuring completeness of audit trails. The cleaning process must preserve essential audit information while managing data volume efficiently.

Regulatory reporting data requires specialized cleaning approaches to ensure compliance with reporting requirements. This involves validating regulatory classifications, ensuring proper jurisdiction assignments, and maintaining accurate regulatory calculations. The cleaning process must handle evolving regulatory requirements while maintaining historical compliance documentation.

The implementation of financial data cleaning processes requires robust control frameworks and clear documentation. Organizations must establish clear data ownership, maintain proper segregation of duties, and ensure adequate review processes. The integration of automated validation rules enhances cleaning efficiency while maintaining control effectiveness.

Success in financial data cleaning ultimately depends on combining technical expertise with deep understanding of financial principles. Organizations must invest in proper tools and training while maintaining clear communication channels between technical and financial teams. Regular review and refinement of cleaning processes ensures ongoing effectiveness in maintaining financial data integrity.

28. Financial Reporting Automation

Financial reporting automation represents a transformative approach to streamlining the preparation and delivery of financial information within organizations. By leveraging Python's powerful data manipulation capabilities, businesses can significantly reduce manual effort while improving accuracy and consistency in their financial reporting processes.

The foundation of effective financial reporting automation lies in establishing standardized data structures and workflows. This involves creating consistent templates for various financial reports, including balance sheets, income statements, cash flow statements, and management reports. Python's pandas library excels at handling these structured financial datasets and maintaining the relationships between different financial elements.

Report generation workflows begin with data extraction and validation. Automated systems pull data from various sources, including accounting systems, ERP platforms, and auxiliary databases. The automation process includes built-in validation checks to ensure data completeness, accuracy, and consistency before report generation begins. This validation layer serves as a critical quality control mechanism.

Financial calculations automation forms a core component of the reporting process. Complex financial metrics, ratios, and KPIs can be calculated automatically using predefined formulas and business rules. The automation system maintains consistency in calculation methodologies while providing flexibility to accommodate changes in reporting requirements or business rules.

Report formatting automation ensures consistent presentation across all financial reports. This includes standardized layouts, fonts, colors, and styling elements. Python libraries like openpyxl and xlsxwriter enable precise control over report formatting, including conditional formatting based on business rules or performance thresholds.

Variance analysis automation provides deeper insights into financial performance. The system automatically calculates and highlights variances against budgets, forecasts, or prior periods. Automated commentary generation can be implemented for significant variances, reducing the time required for initial analysis and allowing finance teams to focus on more strategic insights.

Consolidation reporting automation handles the complexity of multiple entity reporting. The system automatically processes intercompany eliminations, currency translations, and consolidation adjustments. This automation significantly reduces the time and effort required for group reporting while maintaining accuracy in the consolidation process.

Segment reporting automation enables detailed analysis of business performance across different dimensions. The system automatically generates reports by business unit, geographic region, product line, or other relevant segments. This segmentation capability provides valuable insights for business decision making while maintaining consistency in reporting methodologies.

Regulatory reporting automation ensures compliance with various reporting requirements. The system automatically generates reports in required formats for different regulatory bodies, maintaining proper documentation and audit trails. This automation reduces compliance risks while improving the efficiency of regulatory reporting processes.

Management reporting automation provides customized views of financial performance for different stakeholders. The system generates tailored reports for various management levels, incorporating relevant metrics and KPIs for each audience. This customization capability improves the usefulness of financial reports while maintaining consistency in underlying data.

Financial dashboard automation provides real time visibility into key financial metrics. The system automatically updates dashboards with current financial data, enabling proactive monitoring of business performance. These automated dashboards can include interactive elements for deeper analysis and investigation of financial trends.

Report distribution automation ensures timely delivery of financial information to stakeholders. The system automatically generates and distributes reports according to predefined schedules and recipient lists. This automation includes security controls to ensure appropriate access to financial information while maintaining efficient distribution processes.

Exception reporting automation helps identify and investigate unusual financial patterns. The system automatically flags exceptions based on predefined rules and thresholds, enabling focused investigation of potential issues. This automation improves control effectiveness while reducing the time required for routine monitoring activities.

Version control automation maintains proper documentation of report changes and updates. The system tracks modifications to report templates, calculation methodologies, and business rules. This automation ensures transparency in reporting processes while facilitating audit reviews and process improvements.

The implementation of financial reporting automation requires careful consideration of system architecture and integration requirements. Organizations must ensure proper data flows between various systems while maintaining data security and integrity. Regular testing and validation of automated processes ensures ongoing effectiveness of the reporting system.

Success in financial reporting automation depends on close collaboration between finance and technology teams. Organizations must invest in proper training and documentation while maintaining clear communication channels for process improvements and issue resolution. Regular review and refinement of automation processes ensures continued alignment with business needs and reporting requirements.

The future of financial reporting automation lies in the integration of advanced analytics and artificial intelligence capabilities. Machine learning algorithms can enhance anomaly detection and predictive analytics, while natural language processing can improve automated commentary generation. These technological advances will continue to evolve the landscape of financial reporting automation.

29. Marketing Campaign Data Processing

Marketing campaign data processing represents a critical function for modern businesses seeking to optimize their marketing efforts and understand campaign performance. The ability to efficiently process, clean, and analyze marketing campaign data enables organizations to make data-driven decisions and improve their marketing strategies.

Marketing campaign data typically comes from multiple sources, including email marketing platforms, social media advertising, website analytics, CRM systems, and traditional marketing channels. The first step in processing this data involves establishing consistent data collection methods and standardized formats for integration. This standardization ensures that data from different channels can be effectively combined for comprehensive analysis.

Data collection automation forms the foundation of efficient campaign data processing. Python scripts can be developed to automatically pull data from various marketing platforms using their APIs. This automation eliminates manual data collection efforts while ensuring timely and accurate data capture. Regular scheduling of data collection processes maintains up-to-date campaign performance metrics.

Data cleaning and standardization represent crucial steps in marketing campaign data processing. Common challenges include inconsistent naming conventions, duplicate records, and varying date formats across platforms. Python's pandas library provides powerful tools for cleaning and standardizing this data, including functions for text normalization, date parsing, and duplicate removal. The standardization process ensures that campaign data from different sources can be meaningfully compared and analyzed.

Campaign attribution tracking requires sophisticated data processing techniques. Organizations must accurately attribute conversions and customer actions to specific marketing campaigns or touchpoints. This involves processing timestamp data, tracking user interactions across multiple channels, and implementing attribution models. Python's datetime functionality and custom attribution algorithms help manage this complex process.

Cost data processing involves consolidating spending information across various marketing channels. This includes processing invoice data, API cost reports, and manual cost entries. The data processing system must handle different currencies, cost allocation methods, and billing cycles. Automated cost processing reduces manual effort while improving accuracy in campaign ROI calculations.

Audience segment data processing enables better understanding of campaign performance across different customer groups. This involves processing demographic data, behavioral metrics, and custom segment definitions. Python's powerful data manipulation capabilities allow for flexible segment creation and analysis, supporting more targeted marketing efforts.

Campaign performance metrics calculation requires processing raw data into meaningful KPIs. This includes calculating conversion rates, click-through rates, engagement metrics, and custom performance indicators. Automated metric calculations ensure consistency in performance measurement while enabling rapid analysis of campaign effectiveness.

A/B test data processing supports data-driven campaign optimization. This involves processing test group assignments, performance metrics, and statistical significance calculations. Python's statistical libraries provide tools for analyzing test results and determining winning variations. Automated processing of test data enables faster iteration and optimization of marketing campaigns.

Geographic data processing enables analysis of campaign performance across different regions. This includes processing location data, mapping coordinates, and regional categorization. Python's geospatial libraries support sophisticated geographic analysis, helping organizations understand regional variations in campaign effectiveness.

Time-based analysis requires processing campaign data across different temporal dimensions. This includes daily, weekly, and monthly performance tracking, as well as seasonal trend analysis. Python's time series functionality supports complex temporal analysis, enabling better understanding of campaign timing effects.

Channel integration processing combines data from multiple marketing channels to provide a unified view of campaign performance. This involves matching customer identifiers across channels, resolving conflicts in attribution, and creating consolidated performance reports. The processing system must handle different data structures and integration requirements while maintaining data accuracy.

Budget allocation processing supports optimal distribution of marketing resources. This involves processing historical performance data, current budget constraints, and forecasted returns. Python's optimization libraries can help process this data to suggest optimal budget allocations across channels and campaigns.

Creative performance processing analyzes the effectiveness of different marketing creatives. This includes processing image data, ad copy variations, and associated performance metrics. The processing system must handle various creative formats while enabling meaningful comparison of creative performance.

Competitive analysis processing involves handling data about competitor marketing activities. This includes processing market research data, social media mentions, and advertising intelligence. Python's text processing capabilities support analysis of competitive content and campaign strategies.

The implementation of marketing campaign data processing systems requires careful attention to scalability and maintenance. Organizations must ensure their processing systems can handle growing data volumes while maintaining processing speed and accuracy. Regular updates to processing logic accommodate changes in marketing platforms and business requirements.

Success in marketing campaign data processing depends on close collaboration between marketing and analytics teams. Organizations must maintain clear documentation of processing methodologies while ensuring proper training for system users. Regular review and optimization of processing workflows ensures continued alignment with marketing objectives and analytical needs.

The future of marketing campaign data processing lies in the integration of advanced analytics capabilities. Machine learning algorithms can enhance campaign optimization and predictive analytics, while artificial intelligence can improve automated insight generation. These technological advances will continue to evolve the sophistication of marketing campaign data processing systems.

30. Marketing Analytics Workflows

Marketing analytics workflows represent the systematic approach organizations take to transform raw marketing data into actionable insights. These workflows combine data processing, analysis, and visualization techniques to support data-driven marketing decisions and optimize campaign performance across channels.

The foundation of effective marketing analytics workflows begins with clear objective setting and key performance indicator (KPI) definition. Organizations must establish specific metrics that align with their marketing goals, whether focusing on customer acquisition, retention, engagement, or conversion. These KPIs guide the development of appropriate analytical approaches and determine the required data elements.

Data collection workflows form the initial stage of marketing analytics. This involves establishing automated processes to gather data from various marketing channels, including email campaigns, social media platforms, website analytics, and CRM systems. Python scripts can be developed to regularly pull data using APIs, ensuring consistent and timely data availability for analysis.

Data preparation workflows focus on transforming raw marketing data into analysis-ready formats. This includes cleaning operations such as handling missing values, standardizing formats, and removing duplicates. Python's pandas library provides essential functionality for these tasks, enabling efficient data manipulation and standardization. Regular expression operations help clean and standardize text data, while datetime functions process temporal information.

Customer journey analysis workflows map and analyze customer interactions across multiple touchpoints. This involves processing sequential event data, identifying common paths to conversion, and understanding customer behavior patterns. Python's data structures support the organization of complex customer journey data, while visualization libraries help create insightful journey maps.

Campaign performance analysis workflows evaluate marketing effectiveness across channels and campaigns. These workflows process metrics such as conversion rates, engagement levels, and return on investment. Statistical analysis helps identify significant performance trends and factors affecting campaign success. Python's statistical libraries enable sophisticated analysis of campaign results.

Segmentation analysis workflows help organizations understand different customer groups and their responses to marketing initiatives. These workflows process customer attributes and behavioral data to identify meaningful segments. Clustering algorithms implemented in Python help discover natural groupings within the customer base, supporting targeted marketing strategies.

Attribution modeling workflows determine the impact of different marketing touchpoints on conversions. These workflows process multi-channel marketing data to attribute value to various customer interactions. Python's analytical capabilities support different attribution models, from simple last-touch attribution to more complex multi-touch approaches.

Predictive analytics workflows forecast future marketing performance and customer behavior. These workflows process historical data to build predictive models using machine learning techniques. Python's scikit-learn library provides powerful tools for developing and validating predictive models, enabling more proactive marketing decisions.

Budget optimization workflows analyze spending patterns and returns across marketing channels. These workflows process cost and performance data to identify optimal budget allocations. Python's optimization libraries help develop sophisticated allocation models that maximize marketing ROI while respecting budget constraints.

Content performance analysis workflows evaluate the effectiveness of different marketing content types. These workflows process engagement metrics, conversion data, and audience responses to various content pieces. Text analysis techniques in Python help understand content characteristics that drive better performance.

Competitive analysis workflows monitor and analyze competitor marketing activities. These workflows process market research data, social media mentions, and advertising intelligence to understand competitive positioning. Python's web scraping and text analysis capabilities support comprehensive competitive monitoring.

Automated reporting workflows generate regular updates on marketing performance. These workflows process current data to create standardized reports and dashboards. Python's reporting libraries enable automated report generation, while visualization libraries create compelling data presentations.

Real-time analytics workflows process streaming marketing data to enable immediate response to market conditions. These workflows handle continuous data flows from various marketing channels, providing up-to-date performance metrics. Python's streaming data processing capabilities support real-time marketing analytics applications.

Test analysis workflows evaluate the results of marketing experiments and A/B tests. These workflows process test data to determine statistical significance and identify winning variations. Python's statistical testing functions support robust analysis of test results, enabling data-driven optimization decisions.

Marketing mix modeling workflows analyze the effectiveness of different marketing elements. These workflows process historical data to understand the impact of various marketing activities on business outcomes. Python's regression analysis capabilities support sophisticated marketing mix modeling.

The implementation of marketing analytics workflows requires careful attention to documentation and version control. Organizations must maintain clear records of analytical procedures while ensuring reproducibility of results. Python's documentation tools help create comprehensive workflow documentation.

Success in marketing analytics workflows depends on effective collaboration between marketing and analytics teams. Regular communication ensures that analytical insights align with marketing objectives and strategic goals. Continuous workflow optimization helps organizations adapt to changing market conditions and evolving analytical requirements.

The future of marketing analytics workflows lies in increased automation and artificial intelligence integration. Machine learning algorithms will enhance analytical capabilities, while AI-powered systems will provide more sophisticated insights. These technological advances will continue to evolve the complexity and effectiveness of marketing analytics workflows.

Maintaining scalable and efficient marketing analytics workflows requires regular performance optimization. Organizations must ensure their analytical processes can handle growing data volumes while maintaining processing speed. Regular workflow audits help identify opportunities for improvement and optimization.

31. Supply Chain Data Integration

Supply chain data integration represents a critical component of modern business analytics, combining information from multiple sources to create a comprehensive view of the supply chain ecosystem. This complex process requires careful attention to data quality, standardization, and the relationships between different supply chain elements.

The foundation of effective supply chain data integration lies in understanding the diverse data sources involved. Organizations typically need to combine data from enterprise resource planning (ERP) systems, warehouse management systems, transportation management systems, supplier databases, and customer order systems. Each of these sources may use different data formats, naming conventions, and update frequencies, making integration a challenging task.

Data standardization forms the first crucial step in supply chain integration. Organizations must establish consistent formats for key data elements such as product codes, supplier identifiers, location data, and units of measurement. Python's pandas library provides powerful tools for implementing standardization rules across diverse datasets. For example, product codes from different systems can be mapped to a standard format using dictionary-based transformations.

Inventory management data requires particular attention during integration. This includes combining stock levels, reorder points, lead times, and demand forecasts from multiple locations and systems. Python's numerical processing capabilities help normalize inventory metrics across different units and time periods. Time series analysis functions support the alignment of inventory data collected at different intervals.

Supplier data integration involves combining information about supplier performance, pricing, delivery times, and quality metrics. This requires careful handling of hierarchical data structures, as suppliers may have multiple locations, different product lines, and varying service levels. Python's data structures efficiently manage these complex relationships, while its merge functions support the combination of supplier information from different sources.

Transportation data presents unique integration challenges due to its real-time nature and geographic components. Organizations must combine carrier information, routing data, delivery schedules, and tracking updates. Python's geospatial libraries help process location-based data, while its time zone handling capabilities ensure accurate temporal alignment of transportation events.

Order processing data integration connects customer demand with supply chain operations. This involves combining order details, customer information, product specifications, and fulfillment data. Python's data manipulation functions support the creation of comprehensive order views that track items from order placement through delivery.

Cost data integration requires combining financial information from various supply chain activities. This includes procurement costs, transportation expenses, storage costs, and handling fees. Python's numerical processing capabilities support complex cost calculations and allocations across supply chain elements.

Quality control data integration combines inspection results, defect reports, and compliance information from multiple points in the supply chain. This requires careful handling of categorical data and the ability to link quality metrics with specific batches, suppliers, and production runs. Python's statistical functions help analyze quality trends across the integrated dataset.

Forecast data integration combines demand predictions, production planning information, and inventory projections. This requires aligning forecasts from different time horizons and sources while maintaining their statistical properties. Python's forecasting libraries support the combination and validation of multiple prediction sources.

Master data management plays a crucial role in supply chain data integration. Organizations must maintain consistent reference data for products, locations, suppliers, and customers across all systems. Python's data validation functions help ensure the integrity of master data elements during integration processes.

Performance metric integration combines KPIs from different supply chain functions to create comprehensive performance views. This includes metrics for delivery performance, inventory turnover, supplier reliability, and cost efficiency. Python's aggregation functions support the calculation of consolidated performance measures across the integrated dataset.

Real-time data integration capabilities are increasingly important in modern supply chains. Organizations must process streaming data from IoT devices, RFID systems, and real-time tracking systems. Python's streaming data processing capabilities support the integration of real-time information with historical supply chain data.

Data quality management remains essential throughout the integration process. Organizations must implement validation rules, error checking, and data cleansing procedures to maintain the integrity of the integrated dataset. Python's data quality functions help identify and correct inconsistencies across supply chain data sources.

The success of supply chain data integration depends on effective documentation and process management. Organizations must maintain clear records of data sources, transformation rules, and integration procedures. Python's documentation capabilities support the creation of comprehensive integration documentation.

Security considerations play a vital role in supply chain data integration. Organizations must protect sensitive supplier information, pricing data, and customer details while enabling appropriate data access. Python's security libraries help implement data protection measures within integration workflows.

The future of supply chain data integration lies in increased automation and artificial intelligence applications. Machine learning algorithms will enhance data matching and cleansing capabilities, while AI-powered systems will provide more sophisticated integration solutions. These technological advances will continue to evolve the complexity and effectiveness of supply chain data integration processes.

32. Operations Data Management

Operations data management requires a systematic approach to handling the vast amounts of data generated by business operations across manufacturing, service delivery, logistics, and other operational processes. This critical function helps organizations maintain efficiency, identify bottlenecks, and drive continuous improvement through data-driven decision making.

The foundation of effective operations data management begins with establishing clear data collection protocols. Organizations must identify key operational metrics, determine appropriate collection frequencies, and implement reliable data capture methods. This might include automated sensor data from manufacturing equipment, manual entry of quality control measurements, or integrated systems tracking service delivery times.

Data standardization plays a crucial role in operations management. Different departments or facilities often use varying terminology, units of measurement, or recording formats. Using pandas, organizations can implement standardization rules that convert all operational data into consistent formats. For example, production metrics can be normalized to standard units, and time-based measurements can be aligned to a common time zone or reporting period.

Quality control data requires particular attention in operations management. This includes tracking defect rates, process variations, and compliance metrics. Python's statistical libraries enable the calculation of quality control charts, process capability indices, and trend analyses. These tools help organizations monitor operational quality in real-time and identify areas requiring improvement.

Equipment performance data management involves tracking maintenance records, downtime incidents, and efficiency metrics. This data often comes from multiple sources, including equipment sensors, maintenance logs, and operator reports. Python's data integration capabilities allow organizations to create comprehensive equipment performance profiles that support predictive maintenance initiatives and capacity planning.

Workforce productivity data management combines time tracking, output measurements, and skill utilization metrics. Organizations must carefully handle this sensitive data while extracting valuable insights about operational efficiency. Python's data anonymization functions help protect individual privacy while maintaining the analytical value of workforce data.

Process efficiency metrics require the integration of multiple data points to create meaningful performance indicators. This includes cycle times, resource utilization rates, and throughput measurements. Python's calculation capabilities support the creation of complex efficiency metrics that consider multiple variables and operational constraints.

Cost tracking in operations involves managing data about resource consumption, labor allocation, and overhead expenses. Organizations must attribute costs accurately to specific processes, products, or service lines. Python's analytical functions support sophisticated cost allocation models and variance analyses that help identify cost reduction opportunities.

Capacity utilization data management involves tracking the usage of facilities, equipment, and human resources. This requires combining scheduled capacity with actual utilization data to identify optimization opportunities. Python's time series analysis capabilities help organizations understand utilization patterns and forecast future capacity requirements.

Inventory operations data management focuses on tracking raw materials, work in progress, and finished goods throughout the operational process. This includes monitoring stock levels, movement patterns, and storage conditions. Python's data processing capabilities support real-time inventory tracking and optimization of storage allocation.

Service operations present unique data management challenges, requiring tracking of customer interactions, service delivery times, and quality metrics. Organizations must manage both structured data like service times and unstructured data like customer feedback. Python's text processing capabilities help analyze unstructured service data to identify improvement opportunities.

Environmental and safety data management has become increasingly important in operations. Organizations must track energy consumption, waste production, and safety incidents. Python's data validation functions help ensure accurate reporting of environmental metrics and safety statistics while supporting compliance requirements.

Performance reporting requires the consolidation of operational data into meaningful dashboards and reports. Organizations must present complex operational metrics in clear, actionable formats. Python's data visualization preparation functions help create effective operational performance visualizations that support decision making.

Operational risk management data involves tracking incidents, near-misses, and potential hazards. Organizations must maintain detailed records while identifying patterns that could indicate emerging risks. Python's pattern recognition capabilities help identify risk factors in operational data and support proactive risk management.

Continuous improvement initiatives require historical operational data to identify trends and improvement opportunities. Organizations must maintain detailed records of process changes and their impacts. Python's analytical functions support the evaluation of improvement initiatives through before-and-after comparisons of operational metrics.

The future of operations data management lies in increased automation and real-time analytics. Organizations are implementing IoT sensors, automated data collection systems, and real-time monitoring capabilities. Python's streaming data processing capabilities support these advanced operational data management requirements while maintaining data quality and accessibility.

Success in operations data management requires a balanced approach to automation and human oversight. While automated systems can collect and process vast amounts of operational data, human judgment remains essential for interpreting results and making strategic decisions. Python's interactive analysis capabilities support this balanced approach to operations data management.

33. API Data Collection and Processing

API data collection and processing has become a fundamental skill for modern business analytics professionals who need to gather data from various web services, internal systems, and third party platforms. Understanding how to effectively collect, process, and integrate API data enables organizations to build comprehensive data pipelines that provide real time insights into business operations.

The foundation of API data collection begins with understanding the various types of APIs and their authentication methods. REST APIs have become the dominant standard, though SOAP APIs are still encountered in legacy systems. Most modern APIs require authentication through API keys, OAuth tokens, or other security credentials that must be carefully managed within the data collection process.

Python offers several robust libraries for API interaction, with requests being the most widely used. The requests library provides intuitive methods for making HTTP requests and handling responses. When working with APIs, it's essential to implement proper error handling and rate limiting to ensure reliable data collection. This includes catching common HTTP errors, implementing exponential backoff for failed requests, and respecting API rate limits to maintain access.

Data from APIs often comes in JSON format, which requires careful parsing and transformation into structured formats suitable for analysis. Pandas provides powerful tools for converting JSON responses into DataFrames, though nested JSON structures may require custom parsing logic. Organizations frequently need to flatten complex JSON hierarchies while preserving the relationships between different data elements.

Pagination handling is a critical aspect of API data collection, as many APIs limit the amount of data returned in a single request.

Implementing efficient pagination logic ensures complete data collection while minimizing API calls. This often involves tracking pagination tokens or page numbers and implementing loops to collect all available data.

When working with multiple APIs, organizations must handle varying data formats and structures. This requires developing standardized transformation processes that convert data from different sources into consistent formats. Python's data transformation capabilities support the creation of unified data models that combine information from multiple APIs.

API response caching can significantly improve performance and reduce API costs. Organizations should implement caching strategies that balance data freshness requirements with system resource constraints. This might involve storing frequently accessed data locally and implementing cache invalidation policies based on business needs.

Real time data collection through APIs presents unique challenges. Organizations must implement robust streaming data processing pipelines that can handle continuous API updates. This includes managing connection stability, implementing retry logic, and ensuring data consistency across the processing pipeline.

Authentication token management becomes crucial when dealing with multiple APIs or large scale data collection efforts. Organizations must implement secure methods for storing and rotating API credentials. This includes handling token expiration, implementing refresh token logic, and maintaining audit trails of API access.

Data validation for API responses is essential to ensure data quality and consistency. Organizations should implement validation checks that verify response formats, data types, and business rules. This includes checking for missing or invalid data, identifying anomalies, and maintaining data quality metrics.

API version management requires careful attention as APIs evolve over time. Organizations must track API changes, update collection logic as needed, and maintain compatibility with different API versions. This includes documenting API dependencies and implementing version specific handling logic.

Performance optimization for API data collection involves balancing several factors. Organizations must consider network latency, processing overhead, and storage requirements. This might include implementing parallel processing for multiple API calls, optimizing data storage formats, and managing memory usage during large data collections.

Error recovery in API data collection requires robust logging and monitoring systems. Organizations should implement comprehensive logging that captures request details, response data, and error conditions. This supports troubleshooting efforts and helps identify patterns in API failures or data quality issues.

Security considerations in API data collection extend beyond basic authentication. Organizations must implement secure storage for API credentials, ensure secure transmission of sensitive data, and maintain compliance with data privacy regulations. This includes implementing encryption for stored credentials and maintaining access controls for API data.

The integration of API data with other business systems requires careful planning. Organizations must design data models that support efficient querying and analysis while maintaining data lineage. This includes implementing proper indexing strategies, optimizing storage formats, and maintaining metadata about API data sources.

The future of API data collection lies in increased automation and intelligence. Organizations are implementing smart collection systems that can adapt to changing API conditions, optimize collection schedules, and automatically handle common error conditions. This includes developing machine learning models to predict API failures and optimize collection patterns.

Success in API data collection and processing requires a balanced approach to automation and monitoring. While automated systems can handle routine collection tasks, human oversight remains essential for maintaining data quality and addressing complex integration challenges. Organizations must invest in both technical infrastructure and human expertise to build effective API data collection systems.

34. Working with Database Connections

Working with database connections is a critical skill for data professionals who need to interact with enterprise data systems. Modern businesses store vast amounts of data in various database management systems, making efficient and secure database connectivity essential for data analysis and processing workflows.

Database connections in Python are typically handled through specialized database adapters and connection management libraries. The most commonly used library is SQLAlchemy, which provides a comprehensive toolkit for database operations and serves as an Object Relational Mapper (ORM). It supports multiple database backends including PostgreSQL, MySQL, SQLite, and Oracle, allowing organizations to standardize their database interaction code regardless of the underlying database system.

Establishing database connections requires careful consideration of connection parameters and security credentials. Connection strings typically include the host address, port number, database name, and authentication credentials. Best practices dictate storing these sensitive connection details in secure configuration files or environment variables rather than hardcoding them in application code. This separation of concerns enhances security and makes it easier to manage different connection configurations across development, testing, and production environments.

Connection pooling is a crucial concept in database operations, particularly for applications that require frequent database access. Connection pools maintain a set of reusable database connections, reducing the overhead of establishing new connections for each database operation. SQLAlchemy's connection pooling capabilities allow organizations to optimize database access patterns while managing system resources effectively.

Error handling in database connections requires robust implementation to ensure application reliability. Common issues include network timeouts, authentication failures, and connection pool exhaustion. Implementing proper error handling includes catching specific database exceptions, implementing retry logic for transient failures, and maintaining detailed error logs for troubleshooting purposes.

Transaction management is essential when working with databases to maintain data consistency. Python's database libraries provide transaction control mechanisms that ensure atomic operations. Understanding transaction isolation levels and implementing proper transaction boundaries helps prevent data corruption and maintains database integrity during concurrent operations.

Query optimization becomes crucial when working with large datasets or complex database operations. This includes understanding query execution plans, implementing proper indexing strategies, and optimizing query patterns for performance. Python's database libraries often provide query profiling tools that help identify performance bottlenecks and optimization opportunities.

Database connection security extends beyond basic authentication. Organizations must implement proper SSL/TLS encryption for database connections, manage access permissions effectively, and maintain audit trails of database operations. This includes implementing role based access control and monitoring database access patterns for security anomalies.

Working with multiple databases simultaneously requires careful management of connection resources and transaction coordination. Organizations often need to implement distributed transaction management when operations span multiple databases. This includes maintaining transaction consistency across different database systems and handling potential failures in distributed operations.

Large scale data operations often require bulk data transfer capabilities. Python's database libraries provide efficient methods for bulk insert operations and data copying. Understanding these bulk operation patterns helps organizations optimize data transfer performance while maintaining data integrity.

Database schema management becomes important when applications need to work with evolving database structures. Tools like Alembic (often used with SQLAlchemy) provide database migration capabilities that help manage schema changes across different environments. This includes version control for database schemas and automated migration script generation.

Caching strategies play a vital role in optimizing database operations. Implementing proper caching layers can significantly reduce database load and improve application performance. This includes understanding cache invalidation strategies and maintaining cache consistency with the underlying database.

Monitoring database connections and performance metrics helps organizations maintain healthy database operations. This includes tracking connection pool utilization, query performance statistics, and system resource usage. Implementing proper monitoring helps identify potential issues before they impact business operations.

Database connection management in distributed systems presents unique challenges. Organizations must implement proper connection handling across multiple application instances while maintaining consistent database access patterns. This includes managing connection pools in containerized environments and handling database failover scenarios.

Integration with other data processing systems often requires careful coordination of database operations. This includes implementing proper data pipeline stages that interact with databases, managing data consistency across different systems, and optimizing data flow patterns for performance.

The future of database connectivity lies in cloud native database systems and serverless architectures. Organizations are increasingly adopting cloud databases that require different connection management patterns. Understanding these emerging patterns helps organizations build scalable and maintainable database integration solutions.

Success in database connection management requires balancing performance, security, and maintainability. Organizations must invest in proper connection management infrastructure while maintaining flexibility to adapt to changing business requirements. This includes regular review of connection management practices and continuous optimization of database interaction patterns.

35. Cloud Data Sources Integration

Cloud data sources have become increasingly vital for modern business analytics, requiring robust integration strategies to effectively harness data from various cloud platforms. Organizations today rely on multiple cloud services, each offering unique capabilities and data storage solutions that must be seamlessly integrated into analytical workflows.

The foundation of cloud data integration begins with understanding the various types of cloud storage systems. Cloud object storage services like Amazon S3, Google Cloud Storage, and Azure Blob Storage have become the de facto standard for storing large volumes of unstructured data. These services require specific authentication methods and access patterns that differ from traditional file systems.

Python provides several libraries specifically designed for cloud data integration. The boto3 library serves as the primary interface for AWS services, while google-cloud-storage and azure-storage-blob handle Google Cloud and Azure respectively. These libraries abstract away much of the complexity involved in cloud communications while providing robust error handling and retry mechanisms essential for reliable cloud operations.

Authentication and security considerations take center stage when working with cloud data sources. Organizations must implement proper credential management, including role based access control and temporary security tokens. Best practices involve using environment variables or secure credential stores rather than embedding access keys in code. Additionally, implementing proper encryption for data in transit and at rest ensures compliance with security requirements.

Data transfer optimization becomes crucial when working with cloud sources. Implementing parallel download and upload operations can significantly improve performance when dealing with large datasets. Understanding chunked transfer protocols and implementing proper buffering strategies helps optimize memory usage during data transfers. Cloud providers often offer specific tools and APIs for bulk data movement that should be leveraged for optimal performance.

Stream processing patterns play an important role in cloud data integration. Rather than downloading entire datasets, organizations often need to process data streams from cloud sources in real time. Python libraries like smart_open provide streaming interfaces to cloud storage, allowing efficient processing of large datasets without loading them entirely into memory.

Error handling in cloud environments requires special attention due to the distributed nature of cloud systems. Network latency, temporary service unavailability, and throttling limits must be handled gracefully. Implementing exponential backoff strategies and proper error logging helps maintain robust cloud data integration workflows.

Cache management becomes essential when frequently accessing cloud data. Implementing local caching strategies can significantly reduce cloud access costs and improve performance. This includes managing cache invalidation policies and implementing proper cache size limits to prevent local storage overflow.

Cloud data integration often involves working with different file formats and compression methods. Cloud storage services commonly use compression to optimize storage costs and transfer times. Python libraries need to handle various compression formats transparently while maintaining efficient data access patterns.

Data consistency across cloud platforms presents unique challenges. Organizations often need to synchronize data across different cloud providers or between cloud and on premises systems. Implementing proper consistency checks and validation procedures ensures data integrity across distributed storage systems.

Cost optimization becomes a significant consideration in cloud data integration. Cloud providers charge for both storage and data transfer, making it essential to implement cost effective data access patterns. This includes understanding pricing models and implementing strategies to minimize unnecessary data transfers.

Monitoring and logging cloud data operations helps organizations maintain visibility into their integration workflows. This includes tracking transfer speeds, error rates, and cost metrics. Implementing proper monitoring helps identify potential issues and optimize cloud usage patterns.

Version control and data lifecycle management take on new importance in cloud environments. Organizations need to implement proper versioning strategies for cloud data and manage data retention policies effectively. This includes understanding cloud provider specific features for data versioning and lifecycle management.

Integration with existing data processing pipelines requires careful consideration when working with cloud sources. Organizations often need to modify their ETL processes to efficiently handle cloud data sources. This includes implementing proper staging areas and optimizing data movement patterns between processing stages.

Compliance and data governance requirements must be considered when integrating cloud data sources. This includes understanding data residency requirements and implementing proper audit trails for data access. Organizations must ensure their cloud data integration practices align with regulatory requirements and internal governance policies.

The future of cloud data integration lies in serverless architectures and managed services. Cloud providers increasingly offer specialized services for data integration that can significantly reduce implementation complexity. Understanding these emerging patterns helps organizations build scalable and maintainable cloud data integration solutions.

Success in cloud data integration requires balancing performance, cost, and compliance requirements. Organizations must invest in proper integration infrastructure while maintaining flexibility to adapt to evolving cloud services. Regular review and optimization of cloud integration practices ensures continued effectiveness of data analytics workflows.

36. Excel to Python Migration Strategies

Moving from Excel to Python represents a significant shift for many business analysts and data professionals, but this transition offers tremendous benefits in terms of automation, reproducibility, and handling larger datasets. Organizations increasingly recognize the need to modernize their data analysis workflows, making Excel to Python migration a critical strategic initiative.

The migration process begins with understanding the fundamental differences between Excel and Python approaches to data analysis. While Excel provides an intuitive visual interface for data manipulation, Python offers programmatic control and automation capabilities that can dramatically improve efficiency. The key is identifying which Excel workflows would benefit most from Python automation and planning the migration accordingly.

Data import capabilities form the foundation of any migration strategy. Python's pandas library provides robust tools for reading Excel files, including the ability to handle multiple sheets, specified ranges, and various Excel file formats. The read_excel function serves as the primary tool, offering extensive customization options for handling different Excel file structures. Understanding these import capabilities helps ensure smooth data transition between platforms.

Formula translation represents one of the most challenging aspects of Excel to Python migration. Excel formulas must be converted into equivalent Python functions or expressions. Common Excel functions like VLOOKUP can be replaced with pandas merge operations, while complex Excel array formulas often translate to vectorized operations in NumPy. Creating a comprehensive mapping of Excel functions to Python equivalents helps streamline the translation process.

Macro and VBA code migration requires special attention. While Python offers more powerful programming capabilities, the logic embedded in Excel macros needs careful analysis and translation. This often involves breaking down complex macros into smaller functional components and implementing them as Python functions. The process frequently leads to more maintainable and efficient code.

Pivot table functionality, a cornerstone of Excel analysis, finds its Python equivalent in pandas pivot_table and groupby operations. While the syntax differs, Python offers more flexible and powerful aggregation capabilities. Understanding how to replicate common pivot table operations in pandas helps analysts maintain familiar analytical capabilities while gaining additional flexibility.

Data validation and error checking procedures need careful consideration during migration. Excel's built in data validation features must be replicated using Python's data validation libraries or custom functions. This includes implementing input validation, range checking, and custom validation rules that maintain data quality standards.

Visualization migration presents its own challenges. Excel's charting capabilities must be replaced with Python visualization libraries like matplotlib, seaborn, or plotly. While these libraries offer more customization options, the initial learning curve requires careful planning and training. Creating reusable visualization functions helps maintain consistency across reports.

Report automation represents a significant opportunity in Excel to Python migration. Python's ability to generate automated reports, including Excel files, PDFs, and web dashboards, can dramatically reduce manual reporting effort. Libraries like openpyxl enable creation of formatted Excel files, while packages like reportlab support PDF generation.

Performance optimization becomes crucial when handling larger datasets. While Excel struggles with large files, Python offers efficient data structures and processing capabilities. Understanding memory management and optimization techniques helps ensure successful handling of growing data volumes.

User interface considerations play a important role in migration success. Excel users accustomed to interactive interfaces may need alternative solutions. Tools like Jupyter notebooks provide an interactive environment for analysis, while libraries like streamlit or dash enable creation of web based interfaces for data exploration.

Training and documentation requirements cannot be overlooked. Organizations must invest in proper training programs that help Excel users transition to Python. This includes developing documentation that bridges Excel and Python concepts, creating example notebooks, and establishing coding standards.

Version control integration represents a significant advantage of Python based workflows. Unlike Excel files, Python code can be properly version controlled using systems like Git. Implementing version control practices helps maintain code quality and enables collaborative development.

Error handling strategies need careful consideration. Excel's visual error indicators must be replaced with proper Python error handling mechanisms. This includes implementing try except blocks, logging systems, and error reporting mechanisms that maintain robust operation.

Testing and validation procedures ensure accuracy during migration. This includes developing test cases that compare Python results with original Excel calculations, implementing automated testing frameworks, and establishing quality assurance procedures for migrated workflows.

Hybrid approaches often prove useful during transition periods. Organizations may maintain certain processes in Excel while gradually migrating others to Python. Understanding which processes to migrate first and managing the hybrid environment effectively helps ensure successful transition.

Cost benefit analysis helps justify migration efforts. While Python migration requires initial investment in training and development, the long term benefits in terms of automation, reproducibility, and scalability often provide significant return on investment. Documenting these benefits helps maintain organizational support for migration initiatives.

Security considerations change when moving from Excel to Python. While Excel files often contain embedded credentials or sensitive formulas, Python environments can implement proper security practices including credential management and access control. Understanding these security implications helps ensure compliant migration.

Success in Excel to Python migration requires careful planning, proper training, and ongoing support. Organizations must balance the need for modernization with practical constraints while maintaining business continuity. Regular review and optimization of migration strategies ensures effective transition to more powerful and scalable analysis capabilities.

37. Automated Data Validation Systems

Automated data validation systems represent a critical component in modern data processing pipelines, ensuring data quality and reliability across business operations. These systems move beyond simple rule-based checks to implement comprehensive validation frameworks that can automatically detect, report, and often correct data quality issues before they impact business decisions.

The foundation of any automated validation system begins with clear data quality requirements. These requirements must reflect both technical constraints and business rules, encompassing aspects such as data completeness, accuracy, consistency, and timeliness. Successful validation systems translate these requirements into programmatic checks that can be executed automatically and repeatedly.

Data validation in Python leverages several key libraries and frameworks. The pandas library provides built-in validation capabilities through functions like info(), describe(), and isnull(), which offer quick insights into data structure and quality. Custom validation functions can be built using these foundational tools, combined with domain-specific logic that reflects business requirements.

Schema validation serves as a first line of defense in automated systems. Libraries like pandera enable definition of expected data schemas, including column names, data types, and basic validation rules. These schema definitions can be version controlled and shared across teams, ensuring consistent validation standards throughout the organization.

Statistical validation methods add another layer of quality assurance. These include checks for outliers, distribution patterns, and relationship validation between variables. Python's scipy and numpy libraries provide statistical functions that can be incorporated into automated validation workflows, helping identify anomalous patterns that might indicate data quality issues.

Business rule validation implements domain-specific logic that reflects organizational requirements. These rules might include checking for valid customer IDs, ensuring transaction amounts fall within expected ranges, or validating complex relationships between different data elements. Python's flexible programming model allows creation of sophisticated validation rules that can be easily maintained and updated.

Temporal validation becomes crucial when dealing with time-series data. This includes checking for proper date sequences, identifying missing periods, and validating business-specific temporal patterns. Pandas datetime functionality provides tools for implementing these checks efficiently, ensuring temporal data maintains its integrity.

Cross-dataset validation extends quality checks across multiple related datasets. This might involve validating foreign key relationships, checking for consistency in shared reference data, or ensuring balanced totals across different systems. Automated systems can maintain these relationships through scheduled validation checks that identify discrepancies early.

Performance considerations play a vital role in automated validation system design. As data volumes grow, validation checks must execute efficiently to maintain processing windows. Techniques like parallel processing and optimized algorithms help ensure validation systems scale with increasing data volumes while maintaining acceptable performance levels.

Error handling and reporting mechanisms form an essential component of automated validation systems. When validation rules fail, the system must generate appropriate notifications, log detailed error information, and potentially trigger corrective actions. Python's exception handling capabilities combined with logging frameworks enable robust error management.

Validation result storage and analysis helps track data quality trends over time. Organizations often maintain validation result databases that enable analysis of common quality issues, helping identify systematic problems that require attention. This historical perspective aids in continuous improvement of both data quality and validation processes.

Real-time validation capabilities become increasingly important in modern data environments. Python frameworks can implement validation checks that execute as data arrives, preventing invalid data from entering operational systems. This might involve API validation layers, streaming data checks, or database triggers implemented in Python.

Machine learning approaches can enhance traditional validation methods. Anomaly detection algorithms can identify unusual patterns that might indicate data quality issues. Classification models can be trained to recognize valid versus invalid data patterns based on historical examples. These advanced techniques complement rule-based validation approaches.

Configuration management ensures validation rules remain maintainable and adaptable. Rather than hardcoding validation rules, successful systems often implement configuration-driven approaches where rules can be modified without code changes. Python's configuration management capabilities support flexible rule management while maintaining version control.

Integration with workflow systems enables automated responses to validation results. When issues are detected, workflows might include automatic correction attempts, notification of responsible parties, or creation of tickets in issue tracking systems. Python's extensive integration capabilities support connection with various workflow management tools.

Documentation and metadata management become crucial for maintaining validation systems over time. This includes documenting validation rules, their business purpose, and their implementation details. Python's documentation tools and coding standards support creation of maintainable validation system documentation.

Validation system monitoring ensures continuous effective operation. This includes tracking system performance, validation rule coverage, and error detection rates. Monitoring helps identify potential issues with the validation system itself, ensuring it continues to provide reliable data quality assurance.

Testing validation systems requires careful attention to ensure they correctly identify both valid and invalid data conditions. This includes unit testing individual validation rules, integration testing of the complete validation system, and performance testing under expected data volumes. Python's testing frameworks support comprehensive validation system testing.

The future of automated data validation systems points toward increasing sophistication, with artificial intelligence and machine learning playing larger roles in identifying data quality issues. Organizations that implement robust validation systems position themselves to maintain high data quality standards while efficiently handling growing data volumes and complexity.

38. Building ETL Pipelines

Extract, Transform, Load (ETL) pipelines form the backbone of modern data processing systems, enabling organizations to efficiently move and process data from various sources into formats suitable for analysis and decision making. Building effective ETL pipelines requires careful consideration of data sources, transformation requirements, and loading mechanisms while ensuring reliability, scalability, and maintainability.

The foundation of any ETL pipeline begins with the extraction phase. Python offers numerous libraries and tools for connecting to different data sources. The pandas library excels at reading various file formats, while libraries like sqlalchemy provide robust database connectivity. API interactions can be handled through requests or specialized client libraries. Cloud data sources often have dedicated Python SDKs that facilitate data extraction from services like AWS S3, Google Cloud Storage, or Azure Blob Storage.

Data extraction strategies must account for source system limitations and requirements. This includes managing rate limits for API calls, implementing efficient database query patterns, and handling large file downloads. Incremental extraction patterns help manage large datasets by processing only new or changed data since the last extraction. Python's datetime handling capabilities support tracking and managing these incremental loads effectively.

The transformation phase represents the heart of the ETL pipeline, where raw data is converted into the required format for analysis. This often involves multiple steps including data cleaning, standardization, and enrichment. Python's pandas library provides powerful transformation capabilities through operations like map, apply, and transform. Complex transformations can be broken down into discrete steps, making the process more manageable and maintainable.

Data type conversions form a crucial part of the transformation process. This might involve converting strings to dates, handling numeric formats, or standardizing categorical values. Python's strong typing system combined with pandas' data type handling capabilities enables robust type conversion logic. Error handling during type conversion ensures pipeline reliability by appropriately managing conversion failures.

Business rule implementation during transformation ensures data meets organizational requirements. This might include calculating derived values, applying standardization rules, or implementing complex business logic. Python's flexibility allows expression of sophisticated business rules while maintaining code readability and maintainability. Version control systems help track changes to business rules over time.

Data quality checks should be integrated throughout the transformation process. This includes validation of transformed data against expected formats, ranges, and relationships. Python's assertion capabilities combined with custom validation functions enable comprehensive quality control. Failed validations can trigger appropriate error handling mechanisms, ensuring data quality standards are maintained.

The loading phase focuses on efficiently writing transformed data to target systems. This might involve database loading, file writing, or API submissions. Python's database adapters support bulk loading operations for improved performance. When loading to databases, consideration must be given to handling duplicates, managing indexes, and maintaining referential integrity.

Error handling and logging form critical components of ETL pipelines. Python's exception handling capabilities enable graceful management of various failure scenarios. Comprehensive logging helps track pipeline execution, identify issues, and maintain audit trails.

Logging frameworks like Python's built-in logging module or third-party alternatives provide flexible logging capabilities.

Pipeline orchestration manages the sequence and timing of ETL operations. Tools like Apache Airflow, developed in Python, provide robust orchestration capabilities. These tools enable definition of task dependencies, scheduling, and monitoring of pipeline execution. Python-based orchestration frameworks support complex workflow patterns while maintaining code-based pipeline definitions.

Performance optimization becomes crucial as data volumes grow. This might involve implementing parallel processing using Python's multiprocessing library, optimizing memory usage through chunked processing, or leveraging distributed processing frameworks. Careful attention to performance metrics helps identify and resolve bottlenecks in the pipeline.

Testing ETL pipelines requires comprehensive coverage of various scenarios. This includes unit testing individual transformation functions, integration testing of complete pipelines, and performance testing under load. Python's testing frameworks support creation of automated test suites that validate pipeline functionality and performance.

Configuration management enables flexible pipeline behavior without code changes. This includes managing connection strings, transformation rules, and processing parameters. Python's configuration handling capabilities support environment-specific settings while maintaining security of sensitive information like credentials.

Monitoring and alerting ensure timely detection and response to pipeline issues. This includes tracking execution times, success rates, and data quality metrics. Python-based monitoring solutions can integrate with various alerting systems to notify appropriate personnel when issues arise.

Documentation plays a vital role in maintaining ETL pipelines over time. This includes documenting data sources, transformation logic, and loading procedures. Python's documentation tools support creation of comprehensive pipeline documentation that aids in maintenance and knowledge transfer.

Recovery mechanisms ensure pipelines can handle various failure scenarios. This might include implementing checkpoint and restart capabilities, maintaining audit trails for troubleshooting, and supporting data reprocessing when needed. Python's file handling and database capabilities support implementation of robust recovery mechanisms.

Version control and deployment processes ensure reliable pipeline updates. This includes managing code versions, handling database schema changes, and coordinating deployments across environments. Python's packaging tools support creation of deployable pipeline components while maintaining version control.

Security considerations must be addressed throughout the pipeline. This includes securing credentials, implementing appropriate access controls, and protecting sensitive data. Python's security libraries and best practices support implementation of secure ETL processes.

The future of ETL pipeline development points toward increasing automation and intelligence. This might include automated pipeline generation based on source and target metadata, intelligent handling of schema changes, and dynamic optimization of processing patterns. Organizations that implement robust ETL pipelines position themselves to efficiently handle growing data processing requirements while maintaining data quality and reliability.

39. Data Pipeline Optimization

Data pipeline optimization represents a crucial aspect of modern data processing systems, focusing on improving performance, reliability, and resource utilization. As organizations handle increasingly large volumes of data, the need for efficient pipeline operations becomes paramount to maintain processing speed and cost effectiveness while ensuring data quality and timely delivery.

Performance optimization begins with understanding bottlenecks in the data pipeline. This involves comprehensive profiling of pipeline operations to identify time consuming processes and resource intensive tasks. Python's built in profiling tools, such as cProfile and line_profiler, provide detailed insights into code execution patterns. Memory profilers help track memory usage patterns, enabling identification of potential memory leaks or inefficient data handling practices.

Data chunking represents a fundamental optimization technique for handling large datasets. Instead of loading entire datasets into memory, processing data in smaller chunks reduces memory requirements while maintaining processing efficiency. Pandas provides efficient chunking capabilities through its read_csv and read_sql functions with the chunksize parameter. This approach enables processing of datasets that exceed available memory while maintaining consistent performance.

Query optimization plays a crucial role when working with databases. This includes crafting efficient SQL queries, implementing appropriate indexing strategies, and leveraging database specific optimization features. When using SQLAlchemy with Python, understanding query execution plans and utilizing features like bulk inserts and efficient join operations can significantly improve pipeline performance.

Caching strategies can dramatically improve pipeline performance by storing frequently accessed data or intermediate results. Python offers various caching options, from simple in memory caching using dictionaries to more sophisticated solutions like Redis or Memcached. Implementing appropriate cache invalidation strategies ensures data consistency while maintaining performance benefits.

Parallel processing represents a powerful optimization technique for data pipelines. Python's multiprocessing library enables utilization of multiple CPU cores for concurrent data processing. Careful implementation of parallel processing patterns, including proper handling of shared resources and process communication, can significantly reduce processing time for computationally intensive operations.

Distributed processing frameworks extend parallel processing capabilities across multiple machines. Tools like Apache Spark with PySpark enable processing of very large datasets by distributing workloads across clusters. Understanding distributed processing patterns and implementing appropriate partitioning strategies becomes crucial for optimal performance in distributed environments.

Data compression techniques help optimize storage and transfer operations within pipelines. Python supports various compression algorithms through libraries like gzip and bzip2. Selecting appropriate compression methods based on data characteristics and processing requirements can significantly reduce storage costs and transfer times while maintaining processing efficiency.

Pipeline scheduling optimization ensures efficient resource utilization across multiple pipeline runs. This includes implementing appropriate scheduling patterns, managing pipeline dependencies, and coordinating resource allocation. Tools like Apache Airflow enable sophisticated scheduling strategies while maintaining pipeline reliability.

Memory management optimization focuses on efficient use of available memory resources. This includes implementing streaming operations where possible, properly closing file handles and database connections, and utilizing garbage collection effectively. Understanding Python's memory management model helps in implementing memory efficient processing patterns.

Network optimization becomes crucial when pipelines involve data transfer across systems. This includes implementing efficient batch operations, utilizing appropriate protocols for data transfer, and managing network bandwidth usage. Python's networking libraries support implementation of optimized data transfer patterns.

Code optimization at the algorithmic level can significantly improve pipeline performance. This includes selecting appropriate data structures, implementing efficient algorithms, and minimizing computational complexity. Understanding Python's performance characteristics helps in writing optimized code that maintains readability and maintainability.

Database optimization strategies extend beyond query optimization to include proper index management, partition strategies, and maintenance operations. Regular analysis of database performance metrics helps identify optimization opportunities and maintain consistent performance over time.

Error handling optimization ensures pipeline reliability while maintaining performance. This includes implementing appropriate retry mechanisms, managing timeouts effectively, and handling edge cases efficiently. Proper error handling prevents pipeline failures while maintaining processing efficiency.

Monitoring optimization enables proactive performance management. This includes implementing appropriate metrics collection, performance alerting, and trend analysis. Python's monitoring libraries support comprehensive performance tracking while maintaining minimal overhead.

Resource allocation optimization ensures efficient use of computing resources across pipeline operations. This includes managing CPU utilization, memory allocation, and disk I/O operations. Understanding resource requirements helps in implementing appropriate scaling strategies.

Pipeline architecture optimization focuses on overall system design for optimal performance. This includes evaluating pipeline components, optimizing data flow patterns, and implementing appropriate architectural patterns. Regular architecture reviews help identify optimization opportunities and maintain system efficiency.

Testing optimization ensures comprehensive coverage while maintaining efficient test execution. This includes implementing appropriate test strategies, optimizing test data management, and maintaining efficient test environments. Python's testing frameworks support implementation of optimized test suites.

Documentation optimization ensures maintenance efficiency while maintaining comprehensive coverage. This includes implementing appropriate documentation patterns, managing documentation updates efficiently, and maintaining accessibility of pipeline documentation. Python's documentation tools support efficient documentation management.

The future of pipeline optimization points toward increasing automation and intelligence in optimization processes. This includes automated performance tuning, intelligent resource allocation, and dynamic optimization based on workload patterns. Organizations that implement comprehensive pipeline optimization strategies position themselves to handle growing data processing requirements efficiently while maintaining system reliability and performance.

40. Performance Tuning for Large Datasets

Performance tuning for large datasets represents a critical skill in modern data analysis, particularly as businesses increasingly work with massive volumes of information. The challenges of processing large datasets efficiently while maintaining system stability and reasonable execution times require a systematic approach to performance optimization and careful consideration of resource utilization.

Memory management forms the foundation of performance tuning when working with large datasets. Python's memory handling becomes particularly important when dealing with datasets that approach or exceed available RAM. The pandas library, while powerful, can consume significant memory resources due to its design choices and data structures. Understanding how to implement memory efficient operations becomes crucial. For example, using dtype optimization can significantly reduce memory usage by ensuring numerical columns use appropriate data types rather than defaulting to more memory intensive options.

Chunking strategies play a vital role in processing large datasets efficiently. Rather than loading entire datasets into memory at once, processing data in manageable chunks allows for handling of datasets many times larger than available RAM. Pandas provides several approaches to chunking, including the iterator functionality in read_csv and read_sql_query. When implementing chunking, careful consideration must be given to chunk size selection, balancing memory usage against processing overhead.

Generator functions offer another powerful tool for memory efficient data processing. By yielding results one at a time rather than creating large intermediate data structures, generators enable processing of large datasets with minimal memory overhead. This approach proves particularly valuable when implementing data transformation pipelines where not all intermediate results need to be stored simultaneously.

SQL optimization becomes crucial when working with large databases. Understanding query execution plans and implementing efficient query patterns can dramatically improve performance. This includes proper use of indexes, avoiding expensive operations like cross joins, and leveraging database specific optimization features. When working with pandas, using appropriate chunks for SQL queries and implementing server side filtering can significantly reduce memory requirements and processing time.

Vectorization represents a key strategy for improving processing speed with large datasets. Numpy and pandas provide highly optimized vectorized operations that perform significantly better than equivalent Python loops. Understanding how to leverage vectorization effectively, particularly for numerical computations and data transformations, can lead to dramatic performance improvements.

Parallel processing provides another avenue for performance improvement when working with large datasets. Python's multiprocessing library enables utilization of multiple CPU cores for data processing tasks. However, careful consideration must be given to the overhead of process communication and data serialization. In many cases, proper chunking and vectorization may provide better performance than naive parallelization.

Data compression techniques can significantly reduce storage requirements and improve I/O performance when working with large datasets. Python provides various compression options through libraries like gzip and bzip2. When implementing compression, consideration must be given to the tradeoff between compression ratio and processing overhead. Some formats, like parquet, provide both compression and efficient column based access patterns.

Caching strategies become particularly important when working with large datasets that require repeated access to specific portions of data. Implementing appropriate caching mechanisms, whether through memory based caching or disk based solutions, can significantly improve performance for repeated operations. However, careful attention must be paid to cache invalidation and memory management when implementing caching solutions.

Code profiling plays a crucial role in identifying performance bottlenecks when working with large datasets. Python's profiling tools, including cProfile and line_profiler, provide detailed insights into execution patterns and resource usage. Regular profiling helps identify opportunities for optimization and validates the effectiveness of performance improvements.

Data structure selection significantly impacts performance when working with large datasets. Understanding the performance characteristics of different data structures, from pandas DataFrames to specialized structures like sparse matrices, enables selection of appropriate structures for specific use cases. In some cases, using simpler data structures may provide better performance than more feature rich alternatives.

I/O optimization becomes particularly important when working with large datasets. This includes selecting appropriate file formats, implementing efficient reading and writing patterns, and managing disk access patterns. Understanding the performance characteristics of different storage formats and implementing appropriate buffering strategies can significantly improve overall performance.

Resource monitoring provides crucial feedback for performance tuning efforts. Implementing appropriate monitoring of memory usage, CPU utilization, and I/O patterns helps identify performance bottlenecks and validate optimization efforts. Python provides various monitoring tools and libraries that enable detailed resource tracking with minimal overhead.

Error handling requires special consideration when working with large datasets. Implementing appropriate error recovery mechanisms and ensuring efficient handling of edge cases becomes crucial for maintaining processing reliability. This includes implementing appropriate logging and monitoring to track processing issues while maintaining performance.

Testing strategies must adapt when working with large datasets. This includes implementing appropriate test data sampling, validating performance characteristics, and ensuring test coverage of edge cases. Python's testing frameworks provide various tools for implementing efficient testing patterns while maintaining comprehensive coverage.

Documentation plays a crucial role in maintaining optimized code for large dataset processing. This includes documenting performance characteristics, optimization strategies, and resource requirements. Clear documentation enables effective maintenance and further optimization of processing systems over time.

The future of performance tuning for large datasets points toward increasing automation and intelligence in optimization processes. This includes automated performance profiling, intelligent resource allocation, and dynamic optimization based on workload patterns. Organizations that implement comprehensive performance tuning strategies position themselves to handle growing data processing requirements efficiently while maintaining system reliability and performance.

41. Memory Optimization Techniques

Memory optimization techniques represent a crucial aspect of data wrangling in Python, particularly when dealing with large-scale business analytics applications. As organizations process increasingly larger datasets, understanding and implementing effective memory management strategies becomes essential for maintaining system performance and reliability while ensuring efficient data processing.

Understanding Python's memory management system forms the foundation of effective optimization. Python uses reference counting and garbage collection to manage memory automatically, but this convenience can sometimes lead to inefficient memory usage patterns. When working with large datasets, particularly in data analysis workflows, conscious management of memory becomes crucial for maintaining system stability and processing efficiency.

One of the fundamental approaches to memory optimization involves careful data type selection. Pandas DataFrames, while powerful, can consume significant memory due to their flexible nature. Converting columns to appropriate dtypes can dramatically reduce memory usage. For example, using categories for string columns with limited unique values, or downcasting numeric columns to smaller data types when possible, can lead to substantial memory savings without sacrificing functionality.

Memory profiling tools play a vital role in optimization efforts. The memory_profiler library provides detailed insights into memory usage patterns, allowing developers to identify memory intensive operations and optimize accordingly. Regular profiling helps maintain efficient memory usage patterns and identifies potential memory leaks before they become problematic in production environments.

Implementing lazy evaluation patterns represents another powerful memory optimization strategy. Rather than loading and processing entire datasets at once, lazy evaluation allows for processing data only when necessary. Generator expressions and iterators provide mechanisms for implementing lazy evaluation patterns effectively in Python, enabling processing of large datasets with minimal memory overhead.

Data streaming approaches offer significant memory advantages when working with large datasets. Instead of loading entire datasets into memory, streaming allows processing of data in small chunks, maintaining a constant memory footprint regardless of total data size. Libraries like dask provide powerful tools for implementing streaming operations while maintaining a familiar pandas-like interface.

Memory mapped files provide another tool for efficient handling of large datasets. By mapping files directly to memory, this approach allows working with datasets larger than available RAM while maintaining reasonable performance characteristics. The mmap module in Python provides direct support for memory mapped files, while specialized libraries offer higher level abstractions for specific use cases.

Garbage collection optimization becomes particularly important in long running data processing applications. Understanding Python's garbage collection mechanisms and implementing appropriate collection strategies can prevent memory accumulation over time. This includes proper management of circular references and careful handling of large object lifecycles.

Buffer management plays a crucial role in memory optimization, particularly when dealing with I/O operations. Implementing appropriate buffer sizes and managing buffer allocation efficiently can significantly impact overall memory usage patterns. This becomes particularly important when working with multiple data sources or implementing complex data transformation pipelines.

Memory efficient data structures often provide significant optimization opportunities. Using specialized data structures like sparse arrays for datasets with many null values, or implementing custom data structures optimized for specific use cases, can lead to substantial memory savings. Libraries like scipy.sparse provide powerful tools for working with memory efficient specialized data structures.

Caching strategies require careful consideration from a memory perspective. While caching can significantly improve performance for repeated operations, inappropriate caching strategies can lead to excessive memory usage. Implementing appropriate cache invalidation policies and managing cache size effectively becomes crucial for maintaining optimal memory usage patterns.

Database interaction patterns significantly impact memory usage when working with large datasets. Implementing appropriate query patterns, using server side filtering effectively, and managing result set sizes carefully can prevent unnecessary memory consumption. Libraries like SQLAlchemy provide tools for implementing memory efficient database interactions.

Temporary object management represents another important aspect of memory optimization. Creating large temporary objects during data processing can lead to significant memory overhead. Implementing appropriate cleanup strategies and managing temporary object lifecycles effectively helps maintain stable memory usage patterns over time.

Serialization strategies play a crucial role in memory optimization, particularly when implementing distributed processing systems. Choosing appropriate serialization formats and implementing efficient serialization patterns can significantly impact memory usage during data transfer operations. Libraries like msgpack provide memory efficient serialization options for specific use cases.

Error handling patterns require careful consideration from a memory perspective. Implementing appropriate error recovery mechanisms while maintaining efficient memory usage patterns becomes crucial for system reliability. This includes proper management of resources during error conditions and implementing appropriate cleanup procedures.

Testing memory optimization implementations requires specialized approaches. This includes implementing appropriate memory usage validation tests, verifying optimization effectiveness, and ensuring stable memory usage patterns under various conditions. Python's testing frameworks provide tools for implementing comprehensive memory testing strategies.

Documentation of memory optimization strategies plays a crucial role in maintaining efficient systems over time. This includes documenting memory usage patterns, optimization approaches, and resource requirements. Clear documentation enables effective maintenance and further optimization of memory usage patterns as systems evolve.

The future of memory optimization in Python data wrangling points toward increasing automation and intelligence in optimization processes. This includes automated memory usage optimization, intelligent resource allocation, and dynamic optimization based on workload patterns. Organizations that implement comprehensive memory optimization strategies position themselves to handle growing data processing requirements efficiently while maintaining system stability and performance.

42. Parallel Processing in Python

Parallel processing in Python represents a powerful approach to accelerate data wrangling tasks by distributing computational workload across multiple processors or cores. As businesses deal with increasingly large datasets, understanding and implementing effective parallel processing strategies becomes essential for maintaining processing efficiency and meeting performance requirements.

The foundation of parallel processing in Python builds upon several key libraries and frameworks. The multiprocessing module provides a robust foundation for parallel execution, allowing programs to spawn multiple processes and distribute workload effectively. This approach circumvents the limitations of Python's Global Interpreter Lock (GIL), enabling true parallel execution of CPU intensive tasks common in data wrangling operations.

Understanding process based parallelism represents the first step in implementing effective parallel processing strategies. Unlike thread based approaches, process based parallelism creates separate Python interpreters for each process, enabling full utilization of multiple CPU cores. This approach proves particularly effective for CPU bound operations common in data transformation and analysis workflows.

Data partitioning strategies play a crucial role in parallel processing implementation. Effective partitioning ensures balanced workload distribution across available processors while minimizing communication overhead between processes. Various partitioning approaches, from simple chunk based division to more sophisticated workload balancing algorithms, provide options for different processing scenarios.

The concurrent.futures module offers a higher level interface for implementing parallel processing patterns. This abstraction simplifies the implementation of common parallel processing patterns while maintaining fine grained control over execution when needed. The module's executor interface provides a consistent way to manage both process and thread based parallel execution.

Parallel processing in pandas operations requires special consideration. While pandas itself provides limited built in support for parallel processing, libraries like pandarallel enable parallel execution of pandas operations with minimal code changes. This approach allows organizations to leverage existing pandas based workflows while gaining the benefits of parallel processing.

Distributed computing frameworks extend parallel processing capabilities beyond single machine boundaries. Libraries like dask provide sophisticated distributed computing capabilities while maintaining a familiar pandas like interface. This enables organizations to scale their data wrangling operations across multiple machines while maintaining consistent processing patterns.

Communication patterns between parallel processes require careful consideration. Implementing effective communication strategies while minimizing overhead becomes crucial for maintaining processing efficiency. Python's multiprocessing module provides various communication primitives, from simple pipes to more sophisticated queuing mechanisms.

State management across parallel processes presents unique challenges. Implementing appropriate state synchronization mechanisms while maintaining processing efficiency requires careful balance. Various synchronization primitives, from locks and semaphores to more sophisticated coordination mechanisms, provide tools for managing shared state effectively.

Error handling in parallel processing scenarios requires specialized approaches. Implementing robust error recovery mechanisms while maintaining system stability becomes crucial for production environments. This includes appropriate process monitoring, error propagation strategies, and recovery mechanisms for failed processes.

Resource management plays a vital role in parallel processing implementation. Managing memory allocation across processes, controlling CPU utilization, and implementing appropriate resource cleanup procedures ensures stable system operation. Tools like resource pools and process managers provide mechanisms for implementing effective resource management strategies.

Load balancing strategies ensure efficient utilization of available processing resources. Dynamic load balancing mechanisms adapt to changing processing requirements and system conditions, maintaining optimal resource utilization. Various load balancing algorithms provide options for different processing scenarios and workload patterns.

Monitoring parallel processing operations requires specialized approaches. Implementing appropriate monitoring mechanisms while maintaining processing efficiency becomes crucial for system maintenance and optimization. Various monitoring tools and libraries provide options for tracking process status, resource utilization, and processing progress.

Testing parallel processing implementations presents unique challenges. Implementing appropriate testing strategies while maintaining test reliability requires careful consideration. This includes testing for race conditions, deadlock scenarios, and proper resource cleanup under various execution conditions.

Performance optimization in parallel processing contexts requires holistic approach. Understanding interaction between various system components, from CPU and memory utilization to I/O patterns, enables effective optimization strategies. Profiling tools designed for parallel processing scenarios provide insights for optimization efforts.

Documentation of parallel processing implementations plays crucial role in system maintenance. Clear documentation of processing patterns, resource requirements, and coordination mechanisms enables effective system evolution over time. This includes documenting both technical implementation details and operational considerations.

The future of parallel processing in Python data wrangling points toward increasing automation and sophistication. Automated parallelization strategies, intelligent resource allocation, and dynamic optimization capabilities continue to evolve. Organizations implementing effective parallel processing strategies position themselves to handle growing data processing requirements efficiently while maintaining system reliability and performance.

Parallel processing transforms data wrangling operations from sequential execution patterns to distributed processing approaches, enabling efficient handling of large scale data processing requirements. Understanding and implementing effective parallel processing strategies becomes increasingly crucial as organizations deal with growing data volumes and processing requirements.

43. Error Handling and Debugging

Error handling and debugging represent critical skills for developing robust data wrangling solutions in Python. When working with real business data, encountering errors is inevitable due to data quality issues, unexpected formats, resource constraints, and complex processing requirements. Developing systematic approaches to error handling and debugging ensures reliable operation of data processing workflows while enabling efficient problem resolution.

Exception handling forms the foundation of robust error management in Python data wrangling. The try-except pattern allows graceful handling of expected and unexpected errors while maintaining workflow continuity. When processing business data, common exceptions include value errors from invalid data formats, key errors from missing dictionary entries, and type errors from incompatible data operations. Implementing appropriate exception handling ensures processing continues even when individual records contain problematic data.

Defensive programming practices play crucial role in error prevention. Input validation, type checking, and boundary condition testing help catch potential issues before they cause processing failures. When working with business data, validating assumptions about data formats, ranges, and relationships prevents cascading errors that could compromise entire processing workflows.

Logging represents an essential tool for error tracking and debugging. Implementing comprehensive logging strategies provides visibility into processing operations while enabling effective problem diagnosis. Different logging levels, from debug to critical, enable appropriate detail capture for various operational scenarios. Structured logging approaches facilitate automated log analysis and pattern detection.

Error recovery mechanisms ensure workflow resilience in production environments. Implementing appropriate retry logic for transient failures, fallback mechanisms for unavailable resources, and cleanup procedures for partial processing ensures robust operation. Transaction management becomes particularly important when processing involves multiple data sources or storage systems.

Debugging data wrangling workflows requires systematic approach. Understanding common debugging patterns, from print debugging to interactive debugging sessions, enables efficient problem resolution. Tools like pdb provide powerful debugging capabilities while maintaining workflow context. Advanced debugging techniques, including conditional breakpoints and post mortem analysis, help tackle complex issues.

Error aggregation and reporting mechanisms enable effective problem management. Implementing error collection and categorization systems helps identify patterns and prioritize fixes. Regular error analysis reveals systemic issues that might require architectural changes or process improvements. Error reporting automation ensures appropriate stakeholder notification while maintaining operational visibility.

Memory related errors require special attention in data processing contexts. Understanding memory management patterns, from garbage collection to resource cleanup, enables effective handling of memory related issues. Tools for memory profiling and leak detection help identify and resolve memory management problems before they impact production operations.

Performance related debugging presents unique challenges. Identifying bottlenecks, resource contentions, and inefficient processing patterns requires specialized tools and techniques. Profiling tools provide insights into execution patterns while enabling targeted optimization efforts. Understanding interaction between various system components helps resolve complex performance issues.

Integration related errors often emerge when working with multiple data sources and systems. Implementing appropriate error handling for network issues, authentication failures, and protocol mismatches ensures reliable integration operation. Timeout management and circuit breaker patterns provide mechanisms for handling integration failures gracefully.

Data quality related errors require business context awareness. Understanding acceptable data ranges, relationships, and business rules enables appropriate error handling implementation. Data quality scoring systems help identify problematic records while maintaining processing efficiency. Regular data quality monitoring enables proactive issue identification.

Versioning related errors can emerge when handling data from multiple sources or time periods. Implementing appropriate version detection and handling mechanisms ensures consistent processing across different data versions. Schema evolution strategies help manage changing data structures while maintaining processing compatibility.

Configuration related errors often impact data processing workflows. Implementing robust configuration management practices, including validation and versioning, prevents configuration related issues. Environment specific configuration handling ensures consistent operation across development, testing, and production environments.

Documentation plays crucial role in error handling and debugging. Clear documentation of error handling strategies, known issues, and troubleshooting procedures enables efficient problem resolution. This includes documenting both technical implementation details and operational procedures for various error scenarios.

Testing strategies for error handling require comprehensive approach. Unit tests for various error conditions, integration tests for system interactions, and stress tests for resource constraints ensure robust error handling implementation. Chaos engineering practices help identify potential failure modes while enabling proactive improvements.

Monitoring and alerting systems provide operational visibility into error patterns. Implementing appropriate monitoring mechanisms for error rates, processing status, and system health enables proactive issue identification. Alert correlation and aggregation help manage notification volumes while maintaining operational awareness.

The evolution of error handling and debugging practices continues with increasing system complexity. Automated error detection, self healing mechanisms, and machine learning based anomaly detection represent emerging approaches. Organizations implementing effective error handling and debugging strategies position themselves to maintain reliable data processing operations while enabling efficient problem resolution.

Error handling and debugging transform from reactive problem solving to proactive system reliability management. Understanding and implementing effective error handling and debugging strategies becomes increasingly crucial as organizations depend on reliable data processing for business operations. This comprehensive approach ensures robust operation while enabling efficient problem resolution when issues arise.

44. Code Documentation Best Practices

Code documentation serves as a critical foundation for maintainable and collaborative data wrangling projects. Effective documentation practices ensure that code remains understandable, maintainable, and usable by team members across the organization. In the context of business analytics, where data processing workflows often support critical operations, clear documentation becomes even more essential.

Documentation starts with consistent code commenting practices. While Python code should be self-documenting through clear variable names and logical structure, strategic comments provide crucial context about business rules, data assumptions, and processing logic. Comments should explain the why rather than the what, focusing on business context and decision rationale rather than obvious code operations.

Docstrings represent the primary mechanism for Python function and class documentation. Following established docstring conventions, such as Google style or NumPy format, ensures consistency and enables automated documentation generation. Comprehensive docstrings include function purpose, parameter descriptions, return value specifications, and usage examples. For data wrangling functions, documenting expected data formats and handling of edge cases becomes particularly important.

Function level documentation should clearly communicate the business purpose and technical implementation. This includes describing input data requirements, processing assumptions, and output formats. When implementing business logic, documenting the source and validation of business rules ensures long term maintainability. Version information and change history help track evolution of processing logic over time.

Module level documentation provides overview of functionality and usage patterns. This includes describing module purpose, key functions and classes, and typical usage scenarios. Dependencies and installation requirements should be clearly documented to enable smooth deployment. For data processing modules, documenting supported data formats and processing limitations helps prevent misuse.

Project level documentation encompasses both technical and operational aspects. README files serve as the entry point, providing project overview, setup instructions, and usage guidelines. Architecture documentation describes system components and their interactions. Operational documentation covers deployment procedures, monitoring requirements, and troubleshooting guides.

API documentation becomes crucial for reusable data processing components. Clear documentation of public interfaces, including function signatures, parameter specifications, and return values enables effective code reuse. Example code snippets demonstrate typical usage patterns while helping users understand implementation details.

Data documentation forms an essential component of data wrangling projects. This includes documenting data sources, formats, update frequencies, and quality characteristics. Schema documentation describes data structure and relationships. Business glossaries provide context about data fields and their significance in business processes.

Processing workflow documentation ensures operational reliability. This includes documenting data flow between different processing stages, transformation rules, and validation requirements. Dependencies between different processing steps should be clearly documented to enable effective maintenance and modification.

Configuration documentation helps manage system flexibility. Documenting configuration parameters, their purpose, and acceptable values ensures proper system setup. Environment specific configuration requirements should be clearly specified to enable smooth deployment across different environments.

Performance characteristics should be documented to enable effective resource planning. This includes documenting typical processing times, memory requirements, and scaling limitations. Performance optimization opportunities and known bottlenecks help guide future improvements.

Error handling documentation ensures effective problem resolution. Documenting expected error conditions, handling strategies, and recovery procedures enables efficient operation. Error messages should be clearly documented with explanation of causes and resolution steps.

Testing documentation supports ongoing quality assurance. Test coverage, testing strategies, and test data requirements should be clearly documented. This includes documenting both unit tests for individual components and integration tests for complete workflows.

Maintenance documentation enables effective long term operation. This includes documenting regular maintenance procedures, cleanup requirements, and archival strategies. Backup and recovery procedures ensure business continuity in case of failures.

Version control practices should be documented to enable effective collaboration. This includes documenting branching strategies, release procedures, and version numbering schemes. Change management processes ensure controlled evolution of processing logic.

Security considerations require appropriate documentation. Access control requirements, data privacy constraints, and security measures should be clearly documented. Compliance requirements and audit procedures need documentation to ensure ongoing conformance.

Documentation maintenance represents an ongoing requirement. Regular review and updates ensure documentation remains current and useful. Automated documentation generation tools help maintain consistency between code and documentation.

Documentation standards should be established and enforced across the organization. This includes defining documentation requirements for different components, establishing review procedures, and implementing validation mechanisms. Documentation quality metrics help track effectiveness of documentation practices.

The investment in comprehensive documentation pays dividends through improved maintainability, reduced onboarding time, and more reliable operations. As data processing systems grow in complexity, effective documentation becomes increasingly crucial for long term success. Organizations implementing robust documentation practices position themselves for efficient scaling while maintaining operational reliability.

45. Testing Data Wrangling Code

Testing data wrangling code represents a critical aspect of developing reliable and maintainable data processing solutions. In the context of business analytics, where decisions depend on accurate data transformation and analysis, comprehensive testing ensures the reliability of results and protects against costly errors.

Unit testing forms the foundation of a robust testing strategy for data wrangling code. Each data transformation function should be tested independently to verify correct behavior across different input scenarios. Test cases should cover both typical business scenarios and edge cases that might occur in production data. For data cleaning functions, tests should verify handling of missing values, unexpected data formats, and boundary conditions.

Testing data validation rules requires particular attention in business analytics applications. Each validation rule should have corresponding test cases verifying both acceptance of valid data and rejection of invalid data. Tests should cover business rule implementation, ensuring that complex validation logic correctly implements business requirements. Documentation of test cases should clearly link to corresponding business rules for traceability.

Integration testing verifies correct interaction between different components of data processing pipelines. These tests ensure that data flows correctly through multiple transformation stages, maintaining data integrity and business rule compliance throughout the process. Test scenarios should cover end to end workflows, verifying that final outputs meet business requirements when processing real world data volumes.

Performance testing becomes crucial when dealing with large datasets. Tests should verify that processing times remain within acceptable limits as data volume increases. Memory usage patterns should be tested to ensure efficient resource utilization. Performance tests help identify bottlenecks and guide optimization efforts before deployment to production.

Test data management requires careful consideration in data wrangling projects. Test datasets should represent real world data characteristics while maintaining appropriate privacy and security controls. Synthetic data generation techniques can help create comprehensive test scenarios without exposing sensitive information. Version control of test data ensures reproducibility of test results.

Automated testing frameworks streamline the testing process and ensure consistent execution. Python's pytest framework provides powerful features for testing data processing code, including fixtures for test data setup and parametrized tests for checking multiple scenarios. Custom assertions can be developed for common data validation requirements, making tests more readable and maintainable.

Regression testing protects against unexpected changes in data processing behavior. When modifying existing transformation logic, regression tests verify that changes don't impact other aspects of data processing. Automated comparison of results against known good outputs helps identify unintended consequences of code changes.

Error handling testing verifies appropriate behavior under failure conditions. Tests should verify that code handles invalid inputs gracefully, providing meaningful error messages and maintaining data integrity. Recovery procedures should be tested to ensure system resilience in production environments.

Testing documentation practices ensures maintainability of test suites. Test cases should clearly document their purpose, input conditions, and expected results. When testing business rules, documentation should reference relevant business requirements and validation criteria.

Continuous integration practices incorporate automated testing into the development workflow. Tests should run automatically when code changes are committed, providing immediate feedback about potential issues. Test coverage metrics help identify areas requiring additional testing effort.

Mock objects and stubs enable testing of components that interact with external systems. When testing data loading functions, mock objects can simulate database connections or API responses. This allows testing of error handling and edge cases without requiring access to production systems.

Property based testing generates test cases automatically based on defined properties and constraints. This approach can uncover edge cases that manual test case design might miss. For data transformation functions, property based testing can verify that operations maintain required data characteristics across diverse inputs.

Testing data quality checks verifies the effectiveness of data validation frameworks. Tests should confirm that quality metrics correctly identify data issues and that remediation procedures work as intended. Historical quality metrics can be used to verify consistent behavior over time.

Cross validation of results helps ensure accuracy of complex transformations. When implementing new data processing logic, results should be validated against existing systems or manual calculations. Differences should be investigated and documented to confirm correct implementation.

Performance optimization testing verifies the effectiveness of optimization efforts. Benchmarking tests measure improvement in processing speed or resource utilization. These tests should use realistic data volumes to ensure optimizations remain effective in production scenarios.

Security testing verifies that data processing maintains required privacy and security controls. Tests should confirm that sensitive data is properly protected throughout transformation processes. Access control mechanisms should be verified to ensure appropriate restrictions on data visibility.

Testing deployment procedures ensures smooth transition to production environments. Tests should verify that processing logic works correctly with production configuration settings. Environment specific dependencies should be tested to prevent deployment issues.

Maintenance testing verifies ongoing system health. Regular execution of test suites confirms continued correct operation as business requirements and data characteristics evolve. Automated monitoring of test results helps identify emerging issues before they impact business operations.

Code coverage analysis guides testing efforts by identifying untested code paths. While high coverage numbers alone don't guarantee quality, systematic analysis of coverage helps identify gaps in test scenarios. Critical business logic should maintain comprehensive test coverage.

The investment in comprehensive testing practices pays dividends through increased reliability and reduced maintenance costs. As data processing systems grow in complexity, robust testing becomes increasingly crucial for maintaining accuracy and reliability. Organizations implementing systematic testing practices position themselves for confident scaling while maintaining high quality standards in their data wrangling operations.

46. Version Control for Data Projects

Version control stands as a cornerstone of modern data analytics projects, providing essential structure and organization to the development and maintenance of data wrangling code. In business analytics environments, where multiple team members collaborate on data processing pipelines and analysis workflows, effective version control ensures consistency, traceability, and reliability of analytical solutions.

Git has emerged as the standard version control system for data projects, offering powerful features particularly suited to managing data processing code. The distributed nature of Git allows team members to work independently while maintaining a single source of truth for production code. Branch based workflows enable parallel development of features without disrupting stable production systems.

Repository organization for data projects requires careful consideration. Source code for data transformation functions should be organized logically, separating core processing logic from configuration and utility functions. Documentation, including detailed explanations of business rules and data processing assumptions, should be version controlled alongside the code. This ensures that understanding of business logic evolves with the codebase.

Data files present unique challenges for version control. While code files are naturally suited to version control systems, large data files require different strategies. Git LFS (Large File Storage) provides one solution for managing large data files, while other projects might maintain separate data versioning systems. Configuration files pointing to data locations can be version controlled, maintaining reproducibility without storing large datasets in the repository.

Branching strategies should align with business needs and development workflows. Feature branches allow isolated development of new data processing capabilities. Release branches maintain stable versions for production use. Hotfix branches enable rapid response to critical issues while maintaining orderly development processes. Clear branching policies help team members understand how to organize their work effectively.

Commit messages serve as crucial documentation of code evolution. Messages should clearly explain the purpose of changes, particularly when modifying business rules or data transformation logic. References to business requirements, ticket numbers, or documentation help maintain traceability. Atomic commits, focusing on single logical changes, make code history more understandable and facilitate troubleshooting.

Code review processes become more effective with proper version control practices. Pull requests provide a structured mechanism for reviewing changes before they enter production code. Reviewers can examine modifications to data processing logic, verify compliance with business rules, and ensure maintenance of code quality standards. Integration with continuous integration systems enables automated testing of proposed changes.

Version tagging marks significant releases and provides reference points for reproducing specific analysis results. Tags should follow consistent naming conventions and include appropriate documentation of included changes. When analysis results need to be reproduced or audited, tags allow precise reconstruction of the code state used for specific analyses.

Conflict resolution requires particular attention in data projects. When multiple team members modify related data processing logic, careful merging ensures that business rules remain correctly implemented. Version control systems help identify and resolve conflicts, but human understanding of business requirements remains crucial for proper resolution.

Configuration management benefits significantly from version control. Different environments often require different processing parameters or connection settings. Version control helps manage these variations while maintaining consistent core logic. Environment specific configuration can be managed through branches or configuration files, ensuring appropriate settings for development, testing, and production environments.

Dependency management interacts closely with version control. Requirements files listing specific versions of required libraries should be maintained under version control. This ensures reproducibility of analysis environments and helps prevent conflicts between different projects or team members. Virtual environments can be recreated consistently using version controlled dependency specifications.

Documentation workflows should leverage version control capabilities. README files provide essential project information and setup instructions. Technical documentation of data processing logic can be maintained in markup formats, enabling version tracking alongside code changes. API documentation generated from code comments remains synchronized with implementation details.

Collaborative development practices become more effective with proper version control. Team members can work independently on different aspects of data processing while maintaining project coherence. Code sharing and reuse become more manageable when common utilities are maintained in version controlled repositories. Team knowledge sharing improves through detailed commit histories and pull request discussions.

Security considerations influence version control practices. Sensitive information such as access credentials should never be committed to version control. Configuration templates and documentation can guide proper handling of sensitive data while maintaining security. Access controls on repositories help protect proprietary business logic and sensitive code.

Backup and disaster recovery benefit from distributed version control. Multiple copies of repositories provide redundancy, while structured backup procedures ensure no work is lost. Recovery procedures can be tested and documented, providing confidence in system resilience.

Migration and refactoring projects become more manageable with version control. Major changes to data processing logic can be developed and tested in separate branches. Historical versions remain available for reference or rollback if needed. Progressive enhancement of code quality becomes easier to manage and track.

Integration with other tools expands version control benefits. Continuous integration systems can automatically test code changes. Issue tracking systems can link directly to relevant code changes. Documentation systems can pull current information from version controlled sources. These integrations create a comprehensive development environment.

Performance optimization history becomes traceable through version control. Changes made to improve processing efficiency can be tracked and their effects documented. If optimizations cause unexpected issues, previous versions remain available for comparison and rollback.

The investment in proper version control practices pays dividends throughout the lifecycle of data projects. From initial development through ongoing maintenance and enhancement, version control provides structure and reliability to data wrangling workflows. Organizations that embrace comprehensive version control position themselves for sustainable growth and consistent quality in their data processing operations.

47. Reproducible Analysis Workflows

Reproducible analysis workflows form the foundation of reliable and trustworthy business analytics. In today's data-driven organizations, the ability to consistently reproduce analytical results becomes crucial for decision making, audit compliance, and continuous improvement of data processing systems. Creating reproducible workflows requires careful attention to multiple aspects of the analysis process, from data acquisition through final reporting.

The concept of reproducibility extends beyond simple code reuse. A truly reproducible workflow ensures that anyone with access to the necessary resources can obtain identical results by following documented procedures. This includes handling variations in computing environments, managing data dependencies, and maintaining consistent processing parameters. Python's ecosystem provides robust tools for building such reproducible workflows.

Environment management serves as the first pillar of reproducibility. Virtual environments, managed through tools like conda or venv, capture exact versions of required packages and dependencies. Environment specification files should detail all necessary libraries and their versions. Docker containers can provide even stronger isolation, ensuring consistent execution environments across different systems and time periods.

Data versioning plays a crucial role in reproducibility. Input data must be tracked and versioned alongside analysis code. While version control systems like Git handle code effectively, data requires different approaches. Data versioning systems or careful documentation of data sources, including timestamps and version identifiers, help maintain reproducibility. When working with external data sources, mechanisms for capturing and storing specific data versions become essential.

Configuration management ensures consistent parameter settings across different executions. Analysis parameters, file paths, and processing options should be externalized from code into configuration files. These configurations should be version controlled and documented. Different environments might require different configurations, but the underlying analysis logic remains constant. Parameter validation helps prevent subtle variations that could affect reproducibility.

Logging frameworks provide essential tracking of execution details. Comprehensive logging captures important runtime information, including parameter values, processing decisions, and any warnings or unusual conditions. Log files become valuable resources for understanding exactly how results were produced. Structured logging formats facilitate automated analysis of execution histories.

Seed management for random processes ensures reproducibility in analyses involving randomization. Random number generators should be explicitly seeded at well-defined points in the workflow. These seeds should be documented and consistently applied. When multiple random processes occur within an analysis, their interdependencies must be carefully managed to maintain reproducibility.

Documentation plays a central role in reproducible workflows. Beyond code comments, comprehensive documentation should explain the business context, assumptions, and rationale behind analytical choices. Step-by-step execution instructions ensure others can properly run the analysis. Documentation should be maintained alongside code, evolving as the analysis develops.

Modular code organization supports reproducibility by clearly separating different aspects of the analysis. Data acquisition, preprocessing, analysis, and reporting functions should be organized into distinct modules. This organization makes it easier to understand and verify each step of the process. Common utilities can be shared across analyses while maintaining clear dependencies.

Pipeline automation tools help enforce reproducible workflows. Tools like Apache Airflow or Luigi can orchestrate complex analysis pipelines, ensuring consistent execution order and parameter passing. These tools provide monitoring and logging capabilities, helping track successful reproduction of results. Failed steps can be identified and addressed without compromising the entire workflow.

Testing frameworks verify reproducibility at multiple levels. Unit tests verify individual function behavior remains consistent. Integration tests confirm proper interaction between components. End-to-end tests validate complete workflow execution. Regular testing helps identify any changes that might affect reproducibility.

Input data validation ensures consistent starting points for analysis. Automated checks verify data structure, content, and quality metrics. When input data fails validation, clear error messages help identify issues. Valid data snapshots can be preserved to support future reproduction of results.

Intermediate result caching can improve efficiency while maintaining reproducibility. Computationally expensive intermediate results can be cached, but caching mechanisms must preserve full reproducibility. Cache invalidation rules should be clearly defined and documented. Cache contents should be versioned appropriately.

Output validation confirms reproducibility of final results. Automated comparisons can verify that key metrics match expected values. Statistical tests might be needed for results involving random processes. Visualization comparisons can help identify unexpected variations in results.

Error handling in reproducible workflows requires special attention. Error conditions should be clearly documented and handled consistently. Recovery procedures should be defined for common failure modes. Error logs should provide sufficient detail to understand and address issues affecting reproducibility.

Continuous integration systems can automatically verify reproducibility. Regular execution of complete workflows helps identify any issues affecting reproducibility. Integration with version control systems ensures that code changes maintain reproducible behavior. Automated notifications alert team members to reproducibility problems.

Dependency management extends beyond Python packages to include external tools and resources. System dependencies should be documented and verified. External service dependencies must be handled carefully, potentially including mechanisms for mocking or capturing external responses.

Performance optimization must not compromise reproducibility. Optimizations should be implemented in ways that maintain consistent results. Parallel processing implementations must handle random seeds and shared resources appropriately. Performance improvements should be verified through reproducibility testing.

Documentation of results should include reproducibility information. Reports should specify exact versions of code, data, and environments used. Any manual steps or special conditions should be clearly documented. This documentation helps others understand and verify results later.

Regular reproducibility audits help maintain high standards. Periodic verification of complete workflows identifies any drift in results. Documentation and procedures can be updated based on audit findings. These audits build confidence in analytical results and processes.

48. Automated Reporting Systems

Automated reporting systems represent a critical advancement in modern business analytics, transforming how organizations process and share data insights. These systems eliminate manual report generation, reduce human error, and ensure consistent delivery of business intelligence across the organization. The implementation of automated reporting requires careful consideration of multiple components and best practices to create reliable, scalable solutions.

At its core, automated reporting involves creating a systematic process that takes raw data inputs, processes them according to predefined rules, and generates standardized outputs without human intervention. This process begins with data collection mechanisms that can reliably gather information from various sources. These sources might include databases, API endpoints, file systems, or cloud storage solutions. The data collection process must be robust enough to handle connection issues, data format variations, and timing dependencies.

Report scheduling forms a crucial component of automation. Python offers several scheduling frameworks that can trigger report generation at specified intervals or in response to specific events. The schedule library provides a straightforward way to define periodic tasks, while more complex scheduling needs might require tools like APScheduler or integration with system level schedulers. Scheduling logic should account for business hours, data availability windows, and downstream system dependencies.

Template management ensures consistency across generated reports. Report templates define the structure, formatting, and presentation of information. Python libraries like Jinja2 excel at template handling, allowing for separation of content and presentation. Templates should be version controlled and managed centrally to maintain consistency. Dynamic elements within templates must be carefully designed to handle varying data conditions without breaking the report structure.

Data processing for automated reports requires robust error handling and validation. Each step of the data transformation pipeline must include checks for data quality, completeness, and consistency. When anomalies are detected, the system should follow predefined procedures for error notification and fallback behavior. This might include generating partial reports, using cached data, or alerting appropriate personnel.

Output format flexibility allows reports to serve different audience needs. While PDF remains common for formal reports, automated systems often need to generate multiple formats including Excel workbooks, HTML pages, or direct database updates. Libraries like reportlab, openpyxl, and markdown support various output formats. The system should maintain consistent styling and formatting across all output types.

Distribution mechanisms ensure reports reach their intended audiences reliably. Email remains a common distribution channel, with Python's email libraries handling attachment size limits and recipient management. Alternative distribution methods might include uploading to shared drives, posting to internal websites, or integrating with collaboration platforms. Security considerations must guide distribution choices, ensuring sensitive information remains protected.

Performance optimization becomes crucial as reporting systems scale. Techniques like parallel processing can accelerate report generation for large datasets. Caching strategies can reduce redundant calculations across multiple reports. Database query optimization ensures efficient data retrieval. The system should monitor performance metrics and adjust processing strategies accordingly.

Monitoring and logging capabilities provide visibility into the reporting system's operation. Comprehensive logs should track successful report generation, processing times, and any errors or warnings. Monitoring dashboards can display system health metrics and alert on potential issues. Historical performance data helps identify trends and optimization opportunities.

Version control for reporting systems must encompass multiple components. Beyond code versioning, report templates, configuration files, and documentation require careful version management. Changes to report definitions or processing logic should be tracked and reviewed. Version information should be included in generated reports for future reference.

Error recovery procedures ensure business continuity when issues arise. The system should attempt to recover from common failure modes automatically. This might include retrying failed operations, falling back to alternative data sources, or generating simplified report versions. Clear error messages should guide troubleshooting efforts.

Security considerations permeate automated reporting systems. Access controls must protect sensitive data and report contents. Encryption should be applied to stored reports and during transmission. Audit trails should track report generation and access patterns. Regular security reviews help identify and address potential vulnerabilities.

Testing frameworks verify proper system operation. Unit tests confirm individual component functionality, while integration tests verify end to end report generation. Test data sets should cover various edge cases and data conditions. Automated testing helps catch issues before they affect production reports.

Documentation requirements extend beyond technical specifications. Business users need clear descriptions of report contents and interpretation guidelines. Technical documentation should cover system architecture, dependencies, and maintenance procedures. Regular documentation updates ensure continued system supportability.

The success of automated reporting systems ultimately depends on their ability to deliver reliable, timely insights while reducing manual effort and maintaining high data quality standards. Through careful attention to these various aspects, organizations can build robust reporting solutions that scale with their analytical needs.

49. Data Visualization Preparation

Data visualization preparation represents a critical bridge between data processing and effective communication of insights. The process of preparing data for visualization requires careful consideration of data structure, format, and quality to ensure that the resulting visualizations accurately represent the underlying information and effectively convey the intended message to stakeholders.

The foundation of effective visualization preparation lies in understanding the relationship between data structure and visual representation. Different visualization types require specific data formats, and preparing data appropriately can significantly impact the clarity and effectiveness of the final visualization. Time series data, for instance, must be properly indexed and sorted chronologically. Categorical data often needs to be aggregated or transformed to support meaningful comparative visualizations. Numerical data may require normalization or scaling to ensure fair visual comparisons.

Data cleaning takes on additional importance when preparing for visualization. Visual representations can quickly expose data quality issues that might not be immediately apparent in tabular format. Missing values, outliers, and inconsistencies can distort visualizations and lead to misinterpretation. Implementing robust cleaning procedures specifically focused on visualization requirements helps ensure accurate and meaningful visual representations. This might include handling null values appropriately, removing or adjusting extreme outliers, and ensuring consistent categorization across the dataset.

The granularity of data often requires careful consideration during visualization preparation. Raw data may contain more detail than necessary for effective visualization, while sometimes additional calculated fields are needed to support the desired visual representation. Aggregation techniques help manage data granularity, creating summary statistics that can be more effectively visualized. However, care must be taken to preserve important patterns and relationships in the data during aggregation.

Color mapping and scaling decisions often require specific data preparation steps. Continuous variables may need to be binned into categories for effective color mapping. Categorical variables might need to be encoded numerically for certain visualization types. Creating appropriate color scales often involves understanding the distribution of the data and potentially transforming variables to ensure visual effectiveness. This might include log transformations for skewed data or standardization for comparing variables on different scales.

Temporal aspects of data visualization require particular attention during preparation. Time-based visualizations often need specific datetime formatting and handling of time zones. Ensuring consistent time intervals, handling missing time periods, and creating appropriate time-based aggregations are crucial steps in preparation. Seasonal patterns and trends might need to be explicitly calculated to support certain visualization types.

Label preparation plays a crucial role in creating clear and informative visualizations. This involves cleaning and formatting text data that will appear as labels, ensuring appropriate length and readability. Sometimes this requires creating derived fields that combine multiple pieces of information into more meaningful labels. Handling long text strings and implementing appropriate truncation or wrapping strategies ensures labels don't overwhelm the visualization.

Interactive visualization requirements introduce additional preparation considerations. Data must be structured to support rapid filtering and drilling down into details. This might involve creating hierarchical data structures or preparing multiple levels of aggregation. Tooltip content needs to be carefully prepared, often combining multiple fields into meaningful contextual information. The data structure must support smooth transitions between different views or levels of detail.

Performance optimization becomes particularly important when preparing data for interactive visualizations. Large datasets may need to be strategically subsampled or aggregated to maintain responsive performance. Precalculating common aggregations or metrics can improve interaction speed. Careful consideration must be given to the balance between data granularity and visualization performance.

Maintaining consistency across multiple visualizations requires standardized data preparation approaches. This includes consistent naming conventions, consistent handling of special cases, and standardized aggregation methods. When multiple visualizations draw from the same data source, careful preparation ensures they present consistent information and can be effectively combined into dashboards or reports.

Data structure validation becomes crucial when preparing for visualization. Different visualization libraries and tools may have specific requirements for data format and structure. Implementing validation checks ensures the prepared data meets these requirements before visualization attempts. This might include checking for required columns, verifying data types, and ensuring proper indexing.

Documentation of data preparation steps for visualization becomes particularly important when visualizations need to be updated or modified. Clear documentation of transformation steps, aggregation methods, and handling of special cases ensures visualizations can be consistently reproduced and modified as needed. This documentation should include the rationale for preparation decisions to guide future modifications.

The integration of visualization preparation into larger data processing pipelines requires careful planning. Visualization preparation steps should be modular and reusable across different visualization needs. Pipeline design should consider the need to refresh visualizations with updated data, maintaining consistent preparation steps while accommodating changing data content.

Security considerations extend to visualization preparation, particularly when dealing with sensitive business data. Preparation steps must ensure that appropriate data masking or aggregation is applied before visualization to protect sensitive information. This might include anonymizing individual records or implementing minimum group sizes for aggregated data.

The success of data visualization often depends as much on the quality of data preparation as on the choice of visualization type or design. Through careful attention to these various aspects of visualization preparation, analysts can ensure their visualizations effectively communicate insights while maintaining data accuracy and performance requirements.

50. Dashboard Data Processing

Dashboard data processing represents a critical component in modern business analytics, serving as the foundation for interactive and real-time business intelligence solutions. The transformation of raw data into dashboard-ready formats requires specialized processing techniques that balance performance, interactivity, and meaningful business insights.

The fundamental challenge in dashboard data processing lies in structuring data to support multiple, interconnected visualizations while maintaining responsive performance. Unlike static reports or individual visualizations, dashboards typically combine several views of the data that must remain synchronized and interactive. This requires careful consideration of data granularity, aggregation levels, and relationship maintenance between different dashboard components.

Data preprocessing for dashboards often begins with the creation of optimized data structures that support rapid filtering and aggregation. This might involve denormalization of relational data to reduce join operations during dashboard rendering, or the creation of materialized views that store precalculated metrics. The goal is to minimize the computational overhead required when users interact with the dashboard, ensuring smooth and responsive performance even with large datasets.

Aggregation strategies play a crucial role in dashboard data processing. Different levels of aggregation often need to be maintained simultaneously to support various dashboard views, from high-level summary metrics to detailed drill-down capabilities. This requires implementing efficient hierarchical data structures and careful management of aggregation rules to ensure consistency across different dashboard components. The challenge lies in finding the right balance between data granularity and performance requirements.

Real-time and near-real-time dashboard requirements introduce additional complexity to data processing workflows. Data must be structured to support efficient updates without requiring complete recalculation of all dashboard components. This often involves implementing incremental update mechanisms and maintaining appropriate timestamp tracking to ensure accurate representation of the most current data while preserving historical context.

Memory management becomes particularly critical in dashboard data processing. Unlike batch processing scenarios, dashboard data typically needs to remain readily accessible for interactive queries. This requires careful consideration of data storage strategies, potentially implementing caching mechanisms, and managing memory-resident data structures efficiently. The challenge often involves balancing the need for rapid access against memory constraints and system resources.

Filter chain optimization represents another crucial aspect of dashboard data processing. Users typically expect to be able to filter and slice data across multiple dimensions simultaneously, requiring efficient implementation of filter chains that can be applied dynamically without significant performance impact. This might involve preprocessing data to support common filter combinations or implementing optimized indexing strategies for frequently filtered dimensions.

Calculation optimization forms a critical component of dashboard data processing. Complex business metrics often need to be calculated across multiple dimensions and levels of aggregation. Implementing efficient calculation strategies, potentially including precalculation of common metrics or implementation of incremental calculation methods, helps maintain dashboard responsiveness while ensuring accuracy of business metrics.

Data quality management takes on additional importance in dashboard contexts, as data issues become immediately visible to business users. Implementing automated data quality checks and validation procedures as part of the dashboard data processing pipeline helps ensure reliability of dashboard insights. This includes handling of missing values, outlier detection, and consistency checking across different data sources.

Cross-filtering capabilities require special consideration in data processing workflows. The ability to see how selections in one dashboard component affect others requires maintaining appropriate relationships between different data views. This often involves implementing sophisticated data structures that can efficiently support these interactive relationships while maintaining performance.

Temporal aspects of dashboard data often require specialized processing approaches. This might include maintaining different time granularities for different dashboard components, handling time zone conversions, and implementing efficient date-based filtering capabilities. Historical trend analysis capabilities often require specific data structures that can efficiently support time-based comparisons and calculations.

Security and access control considerations must be integrated into dashboard data processing workflows. This often involves implementing row-level security filters and maintaining appropriate data masking or aggregation rules based on user permissions. The challenge lies in implementing these security measures without significantly impacting dashboard performance.

Performance monitoring and optimization become ongoing requirements in dashboard data processing. This includes implementing logging and monitoring capabilities to track dashboard performance metrics, identify bottlenecks, and optimize processing workflows based on actual usage patterns. Regular analysis of these metrics helps ensure dashboard performance meets user expectations over time.

Metadata management plays a crucial role in supporting dashboard functionality. This includes maintaining appropriate descriptions of metrics, dimension hierarchies, and business rules that govern dashboard calculations. Clear metadata documentation helps ensure consistency in dashboard interpretation and supports maintenance of dashboard processing workflows over time.

The integration of multiple data sources often requires specialized processing approaches for dashboard contexts. This might include implementing real-time data integration capabilities, managing different update frequencies across data sources, and ensuring consistency in business metrics across different source systems. Careful attention to data integration processes helps ensure dashboard reliability and accuracy.

As organizations increasingly rely on dashboards for business decision making, the importance of efficient and reliable dashboard data processing continues to grow. Success in this area requires careful attention to performance optimization, data quality management, and implementation of appropriate data structures to support interactive business intelligence capabilities. Through careful consideration of these various aspects, organizations can create dashboard solutions that effectively support business decision making while maintaining necessary performance and reliability standards.

51. Real-time Data Processing

Real-time data processing has become increasingly vital in modern business operations, where organizations need to make decisions based on the most current information available. The ability to process and analyze data as it arrives, rather than in traditional batch processes, enables businesses to respond more quickly to changing conditions and emerging opportunities.

The fundamental concept of real-time data processing revolves around handling data streams as they arrive, typically with minimal latency between data creation and processing. This represents a significant shift from traditional batch processing approaches, where data is collected over time and processed in scheduled intervals. Real-time processing requires different architectural considerations and specialized techniques to maintain both speed and accuracy.

Stream processing forms the backbone of real-time data systems. In Python, libraries like Apache Kafka's Python client, Apache Flink's Python API, and native streaming solutions provide the foundation for building real-time data processing pipelines. These systems must handle continuous data flows while maintaining system stability and ensuring no data loss occurs during processing.

Data windowing strategies play a crucial role in real-time processing. Windows can be time-based, processing all data that arrives within specific time intervals, or count-based, processing fixed numbers of records together. The choice of windowing strategy depends on business requirements and the nature of the data being processed. Time-based windows might be more appropriate for regular business operations, while count-based windows might better serve high-volume transaction processing.

State management becomes particularly important in real-time processing scenarios. Unlike batch processing, where state can be maintained between discrete processing runs, real-time systems must maintain state continuously while processing incoming data. This requires careful implementation of state management strategies, potentially including checkpointing mechanisms to ensure system reliability and recovery capabilities.

Performance optimization takes on new dimensions in real-time processing contexts. The system must maintain consistent processing speeds while handling varying data volumes and potentially complex processing logic. This often involves implementing parallel processing capabilities, careful memory management, and optimization of processing algorithms to minimize latency.

Error handling in real-time systems requires special consideration. Unlike batch processes, where errors can often be handled through reprocessing, real-time systems must handle errors without interrupting the continuous flow of data processing. This might involve implementing sophisticated error handling strategies, including dead letter queues for failed records and automatic retry mechanisms.

Data quality management in real-time contexts presents unique challenges. Traditional batch processing allows for comprehensive data quality checks before processing, but real-time systems must implement quality checks as part of the streaming process. This requires efficient validation algorithms that can operate within the latency constraints of real-time processing while maintaining accuracy.

Monitoring and alerting become critical components of real-time processing systems. Organizations need to implement comprehensive monitoring solutions that track system performance, data quality metrics, and processing latency in real-time. This enables quick identification and resolution of potential issues before they impact business operations.

Scaling considerations must be carefully addressed in real-time processing systems. As data volumes or processing complexity increase, the system must be able to scale efficiently to maintain performance.

This might involve implementing horizontal scaling capabilities, load balancing mechanisms, and efficient resource allocation strategies.

Integration with existing business systems presents another important consideration. Real-time processing systems often need to interact with multiple downstream systems, each with its own requirements and constraints. This requires careful implementation of integration patterns that maintain data consistency while meeting the performance requirements of real-time processing.

Data transformation in real-time contexts requires efficient algorithms that can operate on streaming data. This might include implementing sliding window calculations, running aggregations, and real-time feature engineering for machine learning applications. The challenge lies in maintaining accuracy while meeting the performance requirements of real-time processing.

Security considerations take on additional importance in real-time processing systems. The continuous nature of data flow requires implementing security measures that can operate efficiently without introducing significant latency. This includes real-time encryption, access control, and audit logging capabilities.

Disaster recovery and business continuity planning require special attention in real-time processing contexts. Organizations need to implement appropriate backup and recovery mechanisms that can maintain data consistency and processing continuity even in the face of system failures or other disruptions.

The implementation of real-time processing systems often requires careful consideration of hardware requirements and infrastructure configuration. This might include selecting appropriate processing units, configuring network infrastructure, and implementing caching mechanisms to support the performance requirements of real-time processing.

As organizations continue to move toward real-time decision making, the importance of efficient and reliable real-time data processing continues to grow. Success in this area requires careful attention to system architecture, performance optimization, and implementation of appropriate processing strategies to support business requirements while maintaining necessary performance and reliability standards.

52. Data Privacy and Security

Data privacy and security represent critical considerations in modern data wrangling and business analytics. As organizations collect, process, and analyze increasingly large volumes of sensitive information, the need for robust data protection measures becomes paramount. This chapter explores comprehensive approaches to securing data throughout the analytics lifecycle while ensuring compliance with relevant regulations and industry standards.

Data privacy begins with understanding the nature of the data being processed. Personal identifiable information (PII), financial records, healthcare data, and other sensitive information require specific handling procedures and security controls. Python provides various libraries and tools for implementing these controls, from basic encryption to advanced anonymization techniques.

The first line of defense in data security involves access control and authentication. When working with sensitive data, implementing proper user authentication mechanisms ensures that only authorized personnel can access specific datasets. Python's security libraries offer robust authentication frameworks that can be integrated into data processing workflows. This includes role based access control systems that can restrict data access based on user responsibilities and security clearance levels.

Data encryption serves as a fundamental security measure for protecting sensitive information. Python provides multiple encryption libraries that support both data at rest and data in transit protection. When implementing encryption, it's crucial to consider both the strength of the encryption algorithms and the performance impact on data processing operations. Modern encryption techniques allow for secure data handling while maintaining reasonable processing speeds.

Anonymization and pseudonymization techniques play vital roles in maintaining data privacy while preserving analytical value. These techniques involve transforming sensitive data in ways that prevent individual identification while retaining the statistical properties necessary for analysis. Python offers various methods for data masking, ranging from simple character replacement to sophisticated algorithms that maintain data relationships while obscuring sensitive information.

Data governance frameworks provide structured approaches to managing data security throughout the organization. This includes establishing policies for data classification, handling procedures, retention periods, and disposal methods. When implementing these frameworks in Python, automated tools can help enforce governance policies, track data lineage, and maintain audit trails of data access and modifications.

Secure data transmission represents another crucial aspect of data privacy. When working with distributed systems or cloud services, implementing secure communication protocols ensures data remains protected during transfer. Python's networking libraries support various secure transmission protocols, including SSL/TLS encryption for data in transit.

Compliance with data protection regulations such as GDPR, CCPA, and industry specific requirements demands careful attention to data handling practices. Python based compliance tools can help automate many aspects of regulatory compliance, including data inventory management, consent tracking, and the implementation of data subject rights such as the right to be forgotten.

Audit logging and monitoring form essential components of a comprehensive security strategy. Implementing detailed logging of data access and modifications helps track potential security incidents and demonstrates compliance with security policies. Python logging frameworks can be configured to capture relevant security events while managing log storage and rotation efficiently.

Data minimization principles suggest collecting and retaining only the data necessary for specific business purposes. When implementing data wrangling workflows, this involves carefully considering which data elements are truly required and implementing automated processes to remove or archive unnecessary information. Python scripts can help automate the identification and removal of redundant or unnecessary data.

Secure data disposal presents unique challenges in data analytics environments. Simply deleting files often leaves recoverable traces of sensitive information. Implementing secure deletion methods ensures that sensitive data is properly destroyed when no longer needed. Python provides tools for secure file deletion and data wiping that meet various security standards.

When working with cloud services and third party data processors, additional security considerations come into play. This includes evaluating service provider security controls, implementing proper data sharing agreements, and maintaining visibility into how data is handled by external parties. Python tools can help automate the monitoring and management of cloud service security settings.

Incident response planning becomes crucial for addressing potential security breaches or data exposure events. This includes implementing automated detection systems, establishing response procedures, and maintaining backup systems for critical data. Python based security tools can help automate many aspects of incident detection and response.

Performance optimization while maintaining security requires careful balance. Security measures often introduce processing overhead, but proper implementation can minimize this impact. This might involve selecting appropriate encryption algorithms, optimizing security related code, and implementing efficient security checking procedures that don't significantly impact processing speed.

Regular security assessments and penetration testing help identify potential vulnerabilities in data processing systems. Python security testing frameworks can automate many aspects of security assessment, including vulnerability scanning, code analysis, and security configuration checking.

The future of data privacy and security continues to evolve with new threats and regulatory requirements emerging regularly. Staying current with security best practices and implementing flexible security frameworks allows organizations to adapt to changing security landscapes while maintaining effective data protection measures.

Training and awareness programs play vital roles in maintaining data security. Even the most sophisticated technical controls can be compromised by human error. Developing clear documentation and training materials helps ensure that all team members understand and follow security procedures when working with sensitive data.

53. Best Practices in Production

Best practices in production environments require careful consideration of scalability, reliability, and maintainability when deploying data wrangling solutions. This chapter explores proven approaches for transitioning data processing code from development to production while ensuring robust performance and sustainable operations.

Production readiness begins with code organization and structure. Moving beyond simple scripts, production code requires modular design with clear separation of concerns. This includes organizing data processing functions into reusable modules, implementing proper error handling, and establishing consistent logging practices. Well structured code enables easier maintenance and allows multiple team members to work effectively on the same codebase.

Configuration management represents a critical aspect of production systems. Rather than hardcoding parameters, production code should utilize configuration files or environment variables to manage settings such as database connections, file paths, and processing parameters. Python's configuration management libraries provide flexible solutions for handling different environments while maintaining security.

Version control becomes especially crucial in production environments. Beyond basic code versioning, this includes managing dependencies, documenting API versions, and maintaining compatibility with various data sources. Implementing proper version control practices helps prevent deployment issues and ensures consistent behavior across different environments.

Performance monitoring forms the backbone of reliable production systems. This involves implementing metrics collection for processing times, resource usage, and error rates. Python monitoring libraries can integrate with various monitoring platforms, providing real time visibility into system performance and enabling proactive issue resolution.

Resource management requires careful attention in production environments. This includes implementing proper memory management, connection pooling for databases, and efficient file handling. Production code should gracefully handle resource constraints while maintaining processing efficiency.

Error handling in production must be comprehensive and robust. This involves implementing proper exception handling, providing meaningful error messages, and establishing recovery procedures for different failure scenarios. Automated error notification systems help ensure timely response to processing issues.

Scheduling and orchestration become essential for managing complex data processing workflows. Production systems often require coordinating multiple processing steps, managing dependencies between tasks, and handling retries for failed operations. Python workflow management tools provide powerful solutions for orchestrating complex data processing pipelines.

Documentation practices for production systems extend beyond basic code comments. This includes maintaining detailed API documentation, providing deployment guides, and documenting operational procedures. Clear documentation ensures smooth handoffs between team members and enables effective system maintenance.

Testing strategies for production code must be comprehensive. This includes unit tests for individual components, integration tests for end to end workflows, and performance tests under production like conditions. Automated testing frameworks help maintain code quality while enabling confident deployments.

Deployment procedures require careful planning and automation. This includes establishing clear deployment workflows, implementing rollback procedures, and maintaining separate environments for development, testing, and production. Automated deployment tools help reduce errors and ensure consistent deployments.

Security considerations become paramount in production environments. This includes implementing proper authentication, managing access controls, and protecting sensitive data. Production security measures must balance protection with processing efficiency while meeting compliance requirements.

Backup and recovery procedures ensure business continuity in production environments. This includes implementing regular data backups, maintaining system state information, and establishing clear recovery procedures. Automated backup systems help protect against data loss while enabling quick recovery from failures.

Scaling strategies must account for growing data volumes and processing requirements. This includes implementing horizontal scaling capabilities, managing distributed processing, and optimizing resource utilization. Production systems should scale efficiently while maintaining reliable performance.

Monitoring and alerting systems provide visibility into production operations. This includes tracking system health metrics, monitoring data quality indicators, and establishing alert thresholds. Automated monitoring helps identify issues before they impact business operations.

Code maintenance procedures ensure long term sustainability. This includes regular code reviews, dependency updates, and technical debt management. Establishing clear maintenance procedures helps prevent system degradation over time.

Performance optimization becomes critical at production scale. This includes implementing caching strategies, optimizing database queries, and managing memory usage efficiently. Regular performance testing helps identify optimization opportunities while maintaining system reliability.

Change management procedures protect production stability. This includes implementing proper review processes, maintaining change logs, and coordinating updates across dependent systems. Clear change management helps prevent unexpected issues while enabling necessary system updates.

Disaster recovery planning ensures business continuity. This includes maintaining backup systems, documenting recovery procedures, and regularly testing recovery capabilities. Comprehensive disaster recovery plans help minimize business impact from system failures.

The journey from development to production requires careful attention to numerous operational considerations. By implementing proven best practices and maintaining robust operational procedures, organizations can ensure reliable and efficient data processing in production environments.

54. Case Studies and Real-world Applications

Real world case studies demonstrate how organizations successfully implement data wrangling solutions to solve complex business challenges. Through examining actual implementations across various industries, we can understand practical applications and learn valuable lessons about effective data processing strategies.

Consider the case of a global retail chain that needed to consolidate customer data from multiple regional systems. The challenge involved processing over 50 million customer records from 12 different source systems, each with unique data formats and quality issues. Using Python, the team developed a standardized data processing pipeline that handled various text encodings, normalized address formats, and resolved duplicate customer records. The solution utilized pandas for initial data loading and cleaning, followed by custom matching algorithms implemented with NumPy for efficient processing. Key lessons included the importance of thorough data profiling before standardization and the value of incremental processing for large datasets.

A financial services firm faced the challenge of automating their regulatory reporting process, which previously required manual compilation of data from various trading systems. The solution involved creating an automated ETL pipeline that extracted data from multiple sources, performed necessary transformations, and generated standardized reports. The implementation used pandas for data manipulation, with custom validation rules ensuring data accuracy. The project highlighted the importance of robust error handling and the need for comprehensive audit trails in financial data processing.

In the healthcare sector, a medical research organization needed to clean and standardize patient records from multiple hospitals for a large scale study. The data wrangling solution handled sensitive patient information while maintaining compliance with privacy regulations. The team implemented advanced text processing techniques to standardize medical terminology and used machine learning algorithms to identify potential data quality issues. This case emphasized the importance of domain specific validation rules and the need for careful handling of sensitive data.

A manufacturing company improved their supply chain efficiency by implementing real time data processing for inventory management. The solution integrated data from warehouse management systems, supplier APIs, and transportation tracking systems. Using Python's asyncio library for handling real time data streams, combined with pandas for data transformation, the system provided near real time inventory insights. The project demonstrated the importance of efficient data structures and the need for careful performance optimization in real time processing scenarios.

Marketing analytics provided another compelling case study where a digital advertising agency needed to process campaign data from multiple platforms. The solution consolidated data from social media APIs, web analytics, and customer relationship management systems. Using pandas for data integration and numpy for statistical calculations, the system provided automated campaign performance reports. This implementation highlighted the importance of handling API rate limits and the need for robust error recovery mechanisms.

An energy company's experience with processing sensor data from thousands of smart meters offers insights into handling high volume time series data. The solution involved processing millions of readings daily, implementing efficient storage strategies, and providing real time analytics. Using pandas for initial data cleaning and specialized time series libraries for analysis, the system identified usage patterns and potential equipment issues. This case demonstrated the importance of data sampling strategies and efficient storage solutions for large scale time series processing.

A telecommunications provider successfully implemented customer churn prediction by consolidating and cleaning customer interaction data. The data wrangling solution processed call records, customer service interactions, and billing information to create comprehensive customer profiles. Using pandas for data transformation and scikit learn for feature engineering, the system enabled accurate churn prediction. The project highlighted the importance of handling missing data and the need for careful feature selection in predictive analytics.

These case studies reveal common patterns in successful data wrangling implementations. First, successful projects typically begin with thorough data profiling and quality assessment. Understanding data characteristics and potential issues early helps in designing effective processing strategies. Second, modular design proves essential for maintaining and scaling solutions. Breaking complex processing workflows into manageable components enables easier testing and maintenance.

Performance optimization emerges as a critical factor across cases. Successful implementations carefully consider memory usage, processing efficiency, and scalability requirements. This often involves using appropriate data structures, implementing batch processing where suitable, and utilizing parallel processing capabilities when available.

Error handling and data validation appear consistently important across different industries. Successful implementations include comprehensive validation rules, clear error reporting mechanisms, and robust recovery procedures. This ensures data quality while maintaining processing efficiency.

Documentation and reproducibility also prove crucial for long term success. Well documented solutions enable knowledge transfer and make it easier to maintain and enhance systems over time. This includes documenting data transformations, business rules, and technical implementation details.

Integration capabilities represent another common success factor. Solutions need to handle various data sources and formats while maintaining consistent processing logic. This often involves developing flexible input handlers and standardized data transformation pipelines.

Security and compliance considerations appear particularly important in regulated industries. Successful implementations carefully balance processing requirements with security needs, implementing appropriate access controls and data protection measures.

These real world examples demonstrate that successful data wrangling solutions require careful consideration of business requirements, technical capabilities, and operational constraints. By learning from these experiences, organizations can better prepare for their own data processing challenges and implement more effective solutions.

Don't miss out!

Visit the website below and you can sign up to receive emails whenever George Snypes publishes a new book. There's no charge and no obligation.

https://books2read.com/r/B-A-RNDVC-ENKIF

BOOKS 2 READ

Connecting independent readers to independent writers.

About the Publisher

Northwood Lore Books is an independent imprint dedicated to producing accessible, thought-provoking content through the use of advanced content generation systems. All books published under this imprint are created for educational or entertainment purposes only. Authors listed under this imprint use pen names and are not subject-matter experts. Accordingly, no material should be interpreted as financial, legal, medical, or professional advice. The information provided is general in nature, subject to change, and may not reflect the most current data or guidance. Readers are encouraged to consult official sources or qualified professionals before making decisions based on the content herein.

www.ingramcontent.com/pod-product-compliance
Lightning Source LLC
LaVergne TN
LVHW052315200926
848481LV00002B/571
* 9 7 9 8 2 3 0 4 3 3 9 2 7 *